MOVE YOUR BUS

An Extraordinary New Approach to
Accelerating Success in Work and Life

RON CLARK

TOUCHSTONE

New York London Toronto Sydney New Delhi

Touchstone
An Imprint of Simon & Schuster, Inc.
1230 Avenue of the Americas
New York, NY 10020

First Touchstone hardcover edition June 2015

TOUCHSTONE and colophon are registered trademarks of Simon & Schuster, Inc.

For information about special discounts for bulk purchases,
please contact Simon & Schuster Special Sales
at 1-866-506-1949 or business@simonandschuster.com.

The Simon & Schuster Speakers Bureau can bring authors
to your live event. For more information or to book
an event contact the Simon & Schuster Speakers Bureau
at 1-866-248-3049 or visit our website at www.simonspeakers.com.

Illustrations by Philippe Petit-Roulet

Manufactured in the United States of America

10   9   8   7   6   5

Library of Congress Cataloging-in-Publication Data
Clark, Ron, 1971–
Move your bus : an extraordinary new approach to accelerating success / Ron Clark.
     pages   cm
Includes bibliographical references and index.
    1. Organizational behavior.   2. Organizational effectiveness.   3. Teams in the
workplace—Management.   4. Leadership.   I. Title.
HD58.7.C5196 2015
658.4'09—dc23   2015006675

ISBN 978-1-5011-0503-6
ISBN 978-1-5011-0504-3 (ebook)

For Ryan M. Marshall

I know you are running with the angels, my son.

Contents

Foreword

Sean Covey
Bestselling author of *The 4 Disciplines of Execution*
and *The 7 Habits of Highly Effective Teens*
and executive vice president at FranklinCovey

As business professionals, every day we are faced with challenges. Maybe it's a new manager or customer who we can't seem to please. Or perhaps it's a colleague who seems to be disrupting our best efforts to work together. If you're the boss, you're trying to help your team do more, better, faster, smarter. If you're an employee, you want to do your best work—and get noticed and appreciated for a job well done.

So much of this can seem out of our personal control. But in fact each of us holds the tools necessary to improve ourselves and to help others along the way to, as Ron Clark says, move our own bus. That's why I found this book so crucially important: Ron and his work are propelled by the same spirit of personal accountability and excellence that fuels everything we do at FranklinCovey.

My company has worked with Ron for several years.

He's one of the leading educators in the United States and was named Teacher of the Year in 2000. Ron has gone into classrooms all across the country to talk about his innovative approaches to teaching, which are aligned with Franklin-Covey's Leader in Me school transformation process. He's a world-class educator with a worldwide reputation. But why should we listen to an educator about matters of business? some may ask. Can his lessons from the classroom really inform those of us whose work is usually set in a boardroom or office?

To that I answer a resounding yes. For one thing, Ron is a remarkable businessman. He runs a multimillion-dollar organization, the Ron Clark Academy, considered to be one of the top schools in the world. Every year, he oversees administrative duties large and small and also teaches in the classroom each and every day.

But that doesn't begin to scratch the surface of the work Ron does as the founder and CEO of the Ron Clark Academy. He's constantly fund-raising, organizing events and soliciting donations that bring in millions each year to support his Atlanta school and its students. He's also teaching other education professionals how to do their jobs more effectively, not just his own employees but those at other schools as well. To date, more than twenty-five thousand teachers and principals have gone to the Ron Clark Academy to witness his remarkable teaching methods in person.

To put that into perspective, each day in America, there are one million students sitting in classrooms led by a teacher trained at the Ron Clark Academy.

Business leaders have taken notice. Every year, Ron is invited to share his leadership methods—the same concepts he offers here in *Move Your Bus*—to Fortune 500 companies and other businesses all across the United States and the world. Corporations like FedEx, Xerox, Verizon Wireless, Coca-Cola, Delta Air Lines, BB&T, YP, Turner Broadcasting, Great American Financial, eVestment, and the Federal Reserve have brought Ron in to share his methods with their employees about how to innovate, change, and accelerate success. Somehow, he fits all this work into the same twenty-four hours a day we all have. If that doesn't define a multitasking, multitalented business leader, I don't know what does.

In other words, Ron Clark (in the parlance of this book) is a Runner. His whole life is lived at a flat-out sprint. And he inspires those around him to pick up the pace and run alongside him. Ultimately, this insightful book is all about the relentless pursuit of excellence, in whatever role you may play. If you want to learn how to motivate those around you to run just a bit faster every day—or if you want to learn how to pick up the pace yourself—you must read this book.

Introduction

What does a bus have to do with my business?

The last thing I wanted to do was write this book. I run a world-renowned school that serves as a model for schools and businesses around the world. I teach full-time at the school, with thousands of individuals visiting to watch our staff in action each year. I fund raise to keep the school in operation, and I travel across the globe speaking to schools and businesses about our model of success. I am busier than a centipede at a toe-counting contest. I honestly didn't have time to fit this in, but, while this wasn't a desire, it was certainly a calling. I had to share something we discovered at our school that has the power to transform an organization.

Years ago, I developed an approach to running a business that has electrified leaders and the schools and businesses they run across the country. It started as a simple story about a bus, but it has grown into a massive concept that has led to improved results, morale, and production wherever it is implemented. Before I share this jewel of a story with you, allow me to take a step back and give a frame of reference for what you are about to experience.

Let me tell you an anecdote about a young man in his first job out of school. We'll call him Andy and say he worked for the 3R Organization. Like many people in the business world, Andy had stumbled into a career not really knowing what he wanted to gain from a job or what he hoped to contribute to the organization for which he worked. But as he got started, he was fairly appalled at what he saw. The 3R Organization did not serve its customers very well; it did not provide them with high-quality products and services. And what's worse, the customers had become so used to the shoddy product they paid for that they didn't demand any sort of improvement. Through no fault of their own, they were not very savvy about the goods they were investing their time and money in. They simply didn't know what was possible and had stopped expecting anything better.

Andy didn't yet know a lot about business, but he gradually developed a clear sense that many of the other workers around him were not engaged in their jobs. They came in to work every day and put in their hours, doing the minimum possible to get paid. It was easy for them to coast toward quitting time—and pedal slowly toward retirement—because the customers put so few demands on them. Oh sure, there were customer service issues to work out from time to time, but nothing the average 3R Organization worker couldn't brush under the rug before it was time for a coffee break.

Andy could see that the workers were dragging down the organization. And despite his youth and inexperience, he could look down the road and predict that dire consequences were likely to befall many of these consumers, in ways that could have terrible effects on the entire community. It was a business model that served no one very well. It was a toxic feedback loop of negativity, a crisis just waiting to happen.

So Andy stepped up his game. He had many wild ideas about how better to engage his customers and improve the product they received, and he experimented with implementing even the most farfetched of them. Although his methods were unorthodox, he started to see results. Andy didn't know it at the time, but he was dabbling with a process that the business world today calls *disruptive innovation.*

However, to Andy's mind, his efforts at 3R Organization were just a tiny pinprick of light in the darkness. What he really wanted to do was to light a huge, raging fire under all of the lethargic workers there, not only to inspire them to wake up, but also to shake up the 3R Organization entirely. He dreamed of an organization that hummed with energy and innovation and a culture of excellence. But he was just a midlevel worker himself: he did not have the tools or the power to effect the change he dreamed of for the entire organization. In fact, that would have to wait for another fifteen years, until Andy was at the head of his own organization.

As you may have already guessed, Andy is really me, Ron Clark, and the 3R Organization is a stand-in for the troubled school system I found myself in when I first began my teaching career.

I used these metaphors here as a way to illustrate that *we all face the same high-stakes challenges*, no matter what business sector we work in or what our roles are within an organization. The world moves at lightning speed these days, and we have to keep up as everything evolves around us: technology, culture, consumer preferences, the regulatory environment, societal values—even the climate. As the landscape changes outside of our organizations, we all have to be able to effect change within them. In this book, I'm going to show you how you can do just that.

Two worlds that are not so far apart

Believe it or not, there are many parallels between running a school and running a business. In fact, I often speak to high-level executives at Fortune 500 companies about my strategies for success—in the last few years, I've given talks at Turner Broadcasting, Delta Air Lines, Coca-Cola, BB&T, YP, and Georgia Power, just to name a few companies. Why do these corporate high-flyers want to listen to a teacher? Stay with me as I explain.

Early in my teaching career, I pioneered innovative teaching methods in rural North Carolina that met with great success. This inspired me to pack up my car and move to New York City, where I had heard that the inner-city schools were plagued by low test scores and a critical shortage of skilled teachers. I took on a class of low-achieving students and looked for ways to motivate them: by the end of the year, their test scores were higher than those of gifted students in the same district. This led to recognition as Disney's American Teacher of the Year in 2000, an appearance on *Oprah*, an invitation to the White House, and a *New York Times* best-selling book, *The Essential 55*, in 2003. With proceeds from the book, I founded the Ron Clark Academy, which opened its doors in 2007 in inner-city Atlanta.

Today, more than twenty years after I first stepped foot inside a classroom, I've finally found a way to effect change on a grand scale, the kind of change I'd barely dared to dream about that first year in North Carolina. I run a phenomenally unique school that not only offers a world-class education for children but that also serves as a training site for thousands of administrators and teachers from around the world each year. To put it into perspective, each day in America, there are 1 million children sitting in classrooms led by a teacher who has visited Atlanta and been trained at our Academy. All of those teachers who receive professional development at our school go back to their cities and their classrooms brimming with the same kind of energy, excitement, and passion to educate their students that I had in my first classroom—the kind of energy that I *knew* was possible, if only teachers had the tools to succeed.

Our on-site professional development programs show educators how to be better and show school administrators our secret formula for building a team that creates consistent success at the highest levels. But our programs are also attended by members of the business world who are interested in our methods. Each year these programs raise millions of dollars of revenue that helps to offset the cost required to run the entire organization. In addition to serving as the school's administrator, fund-raiser, and corporate trainer—oh, and I teach in the classroom each day, too!—I also make sixty speeches each year where I share our management methods with other schools and businesses around the world. Those who attend the speeches often want to visit the Ron Clark Academy to see our methods in action and to witness the magic.

The true success of our school is in the success of our students. While more than half of our students come from low-wealth situations, their academic abilities are varied. Before attending RCA, many never had achieved academic success, while others were already performing well. When they graduate, however, they receive millions of dollars in scholarships, and, currently, 100 percent of our graduates are attending college.

The methods we've developed at RCA are effectively inspiring our students and teachers, as well as fostering a culture of excellence at every level. From the youngest student to the most senior administrator, every individual is seeking to accomplish more, to do better, and to succeed at the task before him or her. Sounds like a pretty great environment for a school. In fact, it sounds like an enviable environment for any business.

I'm here to tell you it can happen in your organization— whether you're in a top leadership suite, a tiny office cubicle, or a classroom full of students who will become the leaders of tomorrow. Let this book show you the way.

The miracle of high expectations

Often, the business people I speak to have never considered that education is a complex process, just as business is, or that they share common goals and challenges with me as an educator. Yet, after I have a chance to share these ideas with them, they walk away with a new set of strategies for effective leadership.

So what do I tell them? My key message is to have high expectations of people—because when you do, the people around you *will* meet those expectations. But it's more complicated than that. I believe that all truly inspiring leaders in both the boardroom and the classroom possess one critical piece of knowledge: they know that, in addition to having high expectations of others, they must hold *themselves* accountable for equipping people to meet those expectations. You'll learn more about this as you read on.

When you have high expectations and you push hard and find ways to fire people up, anything is possible. Now the thing is, you can't just set your expectations high and tell people to get there any way they can. If you do that, you guarantee that they will struggle to deliver. Instead, you have to communicate the expectation very specifically and then find ways to uplift people and let them shine.

Here's an example. One of the first things I wanted to change in my classroom in New York City was something that affects everyone, in every part of society: manners. I will say that the kind of common courtesy I was raised with was sorely lacking at my school in Harlem when I arrived. As you can imagine, it would have been completely ineffective to lecture these kids generically about respect and appreciation. So I slowed it down, and I broke it down, and I taught them about manners one simple rule at a time. I literally showed them what I expected. I demonstrated how to give a firm handshake and look people in the eye while speaking to them, how to respond if you accidentally bump into someone and how to eat with proper etiquette, for example, and then we practiced these new manners in the classroom. The children met my expectations every time, and eventually we ended up with 55 simple rules of conduct, which became the basis for my first book, *The Essential 55: An Award-Winning Educator's Rules for Discovering the Successful Student in Every Child.*

Now obviously, this anecdote is about how to educate children, but it's all directly applicable to managing people in the business environment as well. I use the exact same techniques to communicate my expectations to my faculty and staff. They can work for you, too. As a business leader, the more specific you are about your expectations, the more likely your staff, your colleagues, and even your bosses will rise to meet them. And when they don't come through, ask yourself how you can be more specific, more clear, more encouraging. When you develop key leadership behaviors in those around you, you prime them for success, just as I did with my students in Harlem. Trust me: you will achieve your vision one step at a time, the same way I did.

The parable of the bus

During one of my speaking engagements, I used an analogy about a bus to communicate a point about accelerating change within an organization. I did not know at the time that this simple way of looking at an organization would shape my approach to running the Ron Clark Academy, with an eye toward getting the best results possible from my faculty and staff. As I developed the concept further, I saw how much it resonated with my audiences. It is now helping to accelerate change at companies large and small, and I think it can help you, too.

So let me explain the basics. We're going to allow this bus to represent your business. More specifically, it represents the goals and achievements you hope to reach as an organization. Depending on your personal circumstances, the bus could be a corporation, a small business, a sports team, your family, or even a school.

Now, the bus has no gas tank and no gas, because your organization is going nowhere without the people on your team to act as energy and fuel. So imagine that we are going to cut holes in the floorboards and move the bus ourselves, with our own efforts, just like Fred Flintstone did. In other words, the movement of your organization toward its goals depends entirely on the people who are on the team. And that includes YOU. If everyone is performing at the top of his game, success is imminent.

But of course, not everyone is working at the same level when it comes to moving the bus. In every organization, there are different styles of workers, which I mentally categorize by the amount of energy they expend. I think of them as

Runners, Joggers, Walkers, Riders, and Drivers. The Runners are the top performers, the people who really lend their muscle to moving the bus. Joggers are conscientious workers who do a good job but are not at the same level as Runners. Walkers contribute less forward momentum than the others, and Riders are essentially dead weight. We'll learn more about the habits and behaviors of each of them in chapter 1, and you'll be able to determine which style you currently fit into, based on how you contribute to your organization.

Who are you?

- You may be a former Runner who has burned out and is just coasting on the memories of how great you used to be.
- You may be a Walker who wants to run but can't because you are so darn exhausted. The energy to do more just isn't there anymore.
- You may be a potential Runner who is stuck in a situation with a boss who walks and doesn't value your worth to the organization.
- You may be a Rider who wants to be better but has no idea how to begin to walk, much less run.
- You may be a Runner who has looked around and realized that there is a new, younger crop of Runners who seem to be accelerating with turbo boosters that make your run look like a trot.

- You may be a wonderful person who has had horrible things happen to you in your personal life and who feels like the will to run has gone.
- You may even feel as if you have fallen off the bus and been run over by it. For example, you might have received a decrease in pay, added assignments with no compensation or signs of appreciation, or an unwelcome change in your job description (such as, in the case of an educator, a new grade or subject that you will have to teach).

In some of the cases above, you may be less concerned with running than with just getting through the day. I feel you. There have been mornings when I woke up to the alarm clock and felt like there was a ton of bricks holding me down. The thought of getting up and going through the motions of the day was too much to bear.

Remember, I teach in the classroom all day, in addition to acting as the administrator of both the school itself and the educator training program that welcomes hundreds of teachers a week into our building. I have to raise millions of dollars a year to keep our doors open, manage parent and board relations, and deal with the daily "unexpected crazy" that tends to place itself dead-and-center in my path. So sometimes, I wake up thinking *I just can't do it today*. Sometimes it's even worse, and I wake up thinking *I never want to teach again in my life.* But you know, my name is on the building. How can I escape that?

Realizing there is no way out, I pull myself up and head to the shower. I rub Zest soap under my nose and let it sit there. Now, I am not sure if that is healthy or not, but it sure wakes me up. I drive to work and walk into the school building, willing myself to make each step. And as I walk into the building, something always hits me. It's the feeling that keeps me going and that pushes me daily, and I think *I want to be part of something special!*

In the parable of the bus, I am the Driver, and I want to steer my team toward something strong and lasting. I want to make a big difference in the world, to inspire others to reach goals that are meaningful and important. The bus has changed the way I think about work and life—and I promise you it can change your mind-set and your life as well.

Are you ready to get started? This is how it will work. In each chapter, we'll begin with a short fable about how these Runners, Joggers, Walkers, Riders, and Drivers think about their jobs and how they interact with one another in their efforts to move the bus. Some of these fables may seem over-the-top or even a little silly, but that's what allows them to illustrate a point clearly and in a universal fashion. I structured the book this way for a reason.

When I teach history or math or current events, it's all a story. It's about helping people to make connections and delivering information in a way that is clear, engaging, and exhilarating. So when I'm in the classroom and I'm telling my students about Mark Antony's eulogy for Julius Caesar, for example, I'll jump on the desk. The lights are dim. I stand above the students draped in a tunic and as I speak, I encourage the kids to react as they believe the audience would have reacted that day. I want it to come to life, because lessons like that remain in the minds of my students. In much the same way, I wanted to write this book using parables that will resonate with people across industries and job titles. Even though we may all be in different professions, the content of the story unites us.

These are the five characters you'll get to know in our little fables, and their names have been designed to help you to keep their roles straight in your mind as you move through the book.

Cast of Characters

Rufus	The **Ru**nner
Joan	The **Jo**gger
Wanda	The **Wa**lker
Ridley	The **Ri**der
Drew	The **Dr**iver

So read on . . . and get ready for your first ride on the bus!

PART I

Get on the Bus

When I first started teaching, I noticed that some teachers chose to sit at their desks all day while they were teaching. I also saw how the life was sucked out of those classrooms, as the students responded to the lack of movement, energy, and passion. They were like little desk-bound lumps of clay themselves, admonished not to leave their seats or fidget. Other teachers would get up, move around the classroom, and put in a little bit more effort to make their lessons more dynamic. Then there was another whole category of teachers who never slowed down, who had a real pep to their steps. They would be on their feet all day long, bringing a rush of energy to the classroom, flying around the school, dashing to the cafeteria at the end of lunchtime to pick up their students in a fast, up-tempo fashion. Those were the teachers who never seemed tired by dismissal time; they were the ones who were at the school the longest part of the day. They arrived first, and they stayed late for after-school programs. In contrast, the teachers who sat all day would leave at 3:30, as soon as they could. And I gradually came to recognize that the success of the students in each class had a direct correlation to the characteristics of the teacher that they were spending their time with. Energetic teachers were inspiring energetic learners.

So, in my mind, it became almost as if I were in a race. With everything I do, I want it to be different and magical. I'm constantly pushing myself to be the best. I firmly believed that the more energy I brought to the classroom, the more successful my students would be. That notion of a race somehow evolved, in my mind, to the mental image of a long yellow school bus being pushed along by the foot power of the teachers, administrators, and staff. And I started to wonder what would happen if *everyone* on that bus were running as fast as they could. Surely, not only our students, but also our communities and the entire world would benefit if we could move at top speed to inspire our young people and get them tapped into their own potential.

I'm inviting you to imagine your own bus in any size, shape, or color that works for you. Maybe it's not a yellow school bus at all. Maybe it's a long, sleek touring bus with tinted windows that cut the glare or a bright red city trolley with a clanging bell. Maybe it's a double-decker bus that gives you an elevated view of the road in front of you, or an armored bus, or a party bus, or a campaign bus.

Remember, the bus represents your goals and achievements as an organization, which could be anything from your business to your family unit to the committee you chair for your neighborhood association. And don't forget that your bus has no gas tank and is therefore not self-propelled—you're going to pull it along solely with people power.

Are you ready to meet some of the people who might be with you on that bus? Let's go!

1

Runners need support

Rufus is one of the many people pulling that bus. Every day he arrives at the bus depot bright and early, ready to shift into high gear and run like the wind to keep the bus moving forward. As one of those people with a real need for speed, Rufus loves the momentum, the exhilaration of the wind on his face, and the thrill of passing every other bus on the road. Yet, it isn't so much that he wants to cross the finish line first or beat his own personal best. It is more that Rufus longs to be part of something really special, something out of the ordinary—a bus that could fly, perhaps. Oh, it may sound farfetched to you! But Rufus has plenty of ideas about how to make that happen, and he's well known on this bus for his

passion. Rufus can make things happen, and he has a way to
get things done!

Within every type of organization, it is the Runners, like
Rufus, who provide the locomotion. These individuals are
working as hard as possible, and they essentially carry the
load of the bus. They come early or they stay late. They never
complain, and they provide a positive spirit. Their work
ethic is strong, and their attention to detail is spot on. They
are the strongest members of the team, and they are the driving force behind the success of the organization.

Runners are driven by the goal of professional excellence,
and they take pride in contributing to a movement or an en-
tity that is top-notch. Their impetus to work hard is often
less about their personal accomplishments and more about
the good of the organization as a whole. They truly want to
see system-wide success, rather than merely reaping individual accolades, raises, promotions, or awards.

Runners don't let their egos keep them from tackling the
task at hand. They just have an attitude of *It has to be done,
let's knock it out, let's do it*. I witness this at RCA all the time.
For example, recently we were preparing for a big event—
a sneak peek of a beautiful new addition to our school. The
brand-new women's restroom in the newly constructed wing
was on display and part of the tour we were conducting; it
was gorgeously decorated and sparkling clean, so we didn't

want it to be used. But how were we going to make it clear to our guests that the restroom was for viewing only? The easiest way was to make sure all the stalls were locked. One of our teachers, Wade King, said, "I got you." He's a phenomenal educator, he's widely respected, he has been recognized as a District Choice Teacher and Teacher of the Year during his career—and yet he dropped to the floor and was crawling around under all the bathroom stalls to lock the stall doors from the inside. And he was happy to do it! So Runners don't make excuses, and they don't feel above basic tasks. They just want things to get done right.

I spend a lot of time in meetings with corporate executives, including our board members and the corporate sponsors who support RCA. Sometimes I sit back and watch, and I notice a certain way that Runners act in meetings—how they make eye contact with the room, how they don't talk over others. There are some people who know how to lead a meeting so it keeps progressing, and then there are other people who run over other people's ideas and don't add anything of value. Runners have a knack of keeping the meetings moving without missing opportunities. They keep it going, keep it focused, and they recognize the good ideas. And when a Runner is attending a meeting without leading it, he doesn't get in the way of the meeting's forward momentum.

In any organization, the Runners usually prove themselves quickly, so they tend to move up in whatever hierarchy exists in that particular organization. In the corporate world, a top performer is often asked to supervise—and, hopefully, motivate—others, as a first step up the ladder. It's an added responsibility, an added chance to shine by helping others boost their own performance. Big corporations tend to have a clearly defined progression with titles that range from supervisor to department manager to director to vice president. And Runners tend to recognize what they need to do to move up to each level. They're focused, they're driven, but they're also able to stand back and observe, to figure out what it takes to move up.

At our school, it works like this. Every week, hundreds of educators come to watch our teachers in action. We are like the circus, where the greatest act gets the biggest tent. We send visiting teachers to the best spots, the most dynamic classrooms. So when you first start out as a teacher at RCA, you have to prove yourself before you're going to be observed by visitors, or conduct a workshop, or hold court. Our teachers all *want* those visitors in their classrooms. They are pretty much rabid to have more time with the visiting educators because we all share the goal of making a difference in the lives of others. And the Runners figure out what it will take to make that happen.

Unfortunately, Runners tend to devote so much time to their job that they often neglect their personal lives. It's important for leaders to keep in mind that even when their Runners seem happy and appear to be thriving at work, they may be dealing with difficult circumstances at home. If you can tell that your Runners are putting their jobs first, then you need to realize that someone else is most certainly being put second—possibly the Runner's spouse, his friends, or even his children. I have often heard Runners say they feel guilty about spending less time with their own kids in order to contribute to the organization; yet they continue to make the same choice to put their job first. I have also seen Runners neglect their health in their zeal to put the organization first. They eat on the run, go without enough sleep, and often skip their gym appointments in order to sustain their strong work ethic.

As a leader, when you are dealing with these high-achieving Runners, you have to keep in mind the sacrifices they are making. You also have to treat them with some amount of reverence—and by this I mean tempering your criticism and allowing some things to slide, because you don't want to break the spirit of a Runner. If a Runner's spirit is broken, he won't run as fast and, in turn, you will be slowing the entire bus.

And while Runners are indeed the backbone of an organization, they still need support and direction in order to keep up their hectic pace. They may also need some guidance in terms of how to work well with others, particularly their slower colleagues, who may feel some resentment toward them. I have learned a lot about how to manage Runners effectively, and you'll find strategies to do the same as you read on.

I once worked at a school with a teacher who was incredibly negative, even though her students always had extremely high test scores. She complained constantly and was always bad-mouthing the administration. When I developed the parable of the bus, I thought back to that teacher and wondered how to categorize her. She sure had good outcomes, but her demeanor was that of a pessimist; she certainly didn't uplift anyone around her. So was she a Runner or a Walker? I finally decided that she was a Runner going in the wrong direction! If you have a high-performing negative force in your organization, that can be even worse than a having a Walker on your team, because that person may be forcing the bus to go backward.

It is very tempting just to let Runners do their thing and pay very little attention to them. After all, they do the most for the organization, they seem to be heading in the right direction, and it's much more tempting to focus your energies on the problem areas, not the areas where you're seeing success already. But this is actually not the best strategy for dealing with Runners, as we will find out just ahead.

2

Joggers want validation

Joan has a great job on the bus, and she just knows that she does it very well. She is steady and methodical. She pulls the bus along at a brisk yet carefully controlled pace; no one has to give her a boost! Joan knows every safety procedure on every checklist well—after all, that is part of her job description. Occasionally, the bus driver asks her to develop a new safety protocol, and she is okay with doing extra work like that because she always receives praise for it and, hey, it makes her look good! If there is one thing that rattles Joan just a tiny bit, it is that guy Rufus. When she arrives at the depot every morning, he is already there, flexing his muscles and doing something that seems a bit unnecessary, like pol-

*ishing the bus. She likes and respects Rufus, but sometimes
she wonders if he is a bit of a show-off.*

In the big picture, Joggers aren't really hurting anything.
They are steady and dependable; they do their jobs and have
some amount of success. They tend to be fairly punctual and
conscientious about following the rules. Joggers really do
try to keep up, and while they will occasionally break into
a sprint, they simply don't maintain that high level of effort
over the long haul. They don't slow the bus down, but they
don't make it fly either. They definitely contribute to the
forward momentum of the bus—although at a slower pace
than Runners do—and for that reason they are valuable to
an organization.

Joggers will usually meet basic expectations about things
like being on time, meeting deadlines, and being dressed
appropriately for the occasion. They will often even rise to
meet certain high expectations, like coordinating a special
project in a stellar fashion. But they really do not exceed
expectations on a regular basis. They simply aren't going to
blow your mind, day in and day out. And in some instances,
that may be okay.

In education, there's a certain stereotype about coaches
that illustrates what I'm trying to say about Joggers. I don't
mean to throw coaches under the bus, but there's a general
perception among educators that not every high school

basketball or football coach is also the best educator, so he's just kind of coasting along in his teaching duties—until it's time for that big game. Then the coach is killing it, going for the win, screaming from the sidelines, finding ways to motivate his players and carry the team to victory. It's always amazing to me when I see a coach inspire his players to improve or excel on the football field or the basketball court, but I'll admit it's rare that I see the same coach carry that sort of intensity over into his classroom.

So you've got people like this who can switch into high gear when they're called upon to do so or when the stakes are high, but they don't always perform at that level. That's the hallmark of a Jogger. Often they do okay for themselves. In the business world, there are many job positions that can be filled quite adequately with Joggers who can accelerate as needed to close that big sale, pull off a spectacular fundraising gala, or get the quarterly financial report written, designed, and printed on time. And let's face it: there are times when a business leader might find that sort of trade-off acceptable or even advantageous in advancing certain organizational goals. To go back to my coaching analogy, if your school is already known around the world for academic excellence but you lack a championship-winning basketball team, who are you going to hire? And how will you evaluate that person's job performance? It sometimes comes down to a balancing act, where you have to juggle competing interests. I wish everyone on my bus could be a Runner, but I know that isn't realistic.

One curious thing I've noticed about Joggers is that they honestly feel they are doing the best that could ever be expected of anyone, because they are fairly meticulous about performing the tasks they were hired to do. This might be because most Joggers are not inherently lazy, but rather lack a bit of confidence about their abilities—or perhaps tend to pour most of their energy into the tasks they're already the most skilled at and confident about, while coasting through the others. It may also be that Joggers place a higher value than Runners do on work-life balance and are reluctant to let their personal lives slide in order to advance their organization. In many cases, however, and depending on the environment they work in, Joggers may fall just short of the desired performance because they don't often go above and beyond the duties outlined in their job descriptions.

Yet, invariably, if you ask a Jogger where she fits into the organization, she will swear she is a Runner. Sometimes I'll be doing a book signing after speaking to a group of educators, and a teacher will say to me, "Hey, you know that story you told about that bus? Well, I'm one of those Runners." And I'll think to myself, *Hmm, Jogger*. I'm not trying to be snarky here. I figure they're Joggers because Runners don't feel the need to let everyone know they're top performers; Runners make their contributions to the organization because they want to improve the whole, not because they are looking for praise or attention. I've found that Joggers often desperately want to be recognized as Runners, even though they really aren't. They tend to have a burning need for validation from others.

So, for example, RCA once hosted a major corporate event at our school in Atlanta. Attended by our current corporate sponsors and potential corporate supporters, it included business executives from all over the country. This event required months of planning and effort, in part because it was decorated so elaborately, and my entire staff worked exceedingly hard on this immense, ambitious project. At the event that evening, my Runners did a phenomenal job of mingling, talking with guests, making that emotional connection with people. I love my Runners because they're good conversationalists who know how to listen and to say, "Tell me more about you." But I also noticed a Jogger there, someone who had worked very hard on the event, and her conversations that evening were centered on the effort she had put into some specific aspects of the decorations. She was pointing out to the corporate sponsors what she had done. So for her, it wasn't about the event or building strong relationships with corporate sponsors; it was more about "Let me tell you how hard it was to make this happen!"

Joggers often take on one large project every year, and

while they are immersed in that project they very much want everyone to notice that they are doing something that requires special effort. They seek attention for that project not because it helps the organization but because they have a strong personal desire to be recognized for doing something above and beyond basic job requirements.

In the education world, there's a running joke about these one-big-project-per-year teachers, who I think of as the Egg Hatchers. So, for instance, if you're a third-grade teacher, every year your current students might do a science project that involves carefully incubating hen's eggs until the chicks hatch and then caring for the chicks in the classroom. When that first little chicken starts pecking its way through the shell, it's like everything else has to stop, because this is big news. Sometimes the teacher will even make an announcement to the entire school over the intercom that the eggs have hatched. It's a great project for the kids, but it's often the only time of the year that this teacher does anything out of the ordinary to get the students excited and involved in hands-on learning. Still, that egg hatching is her thing, and she owns it, she wants to be known for it—no matter that there are many other good projects out there to get younger students involved in science. This is a classic example of a Jogger.

I see "egg hatchers" in the business world as well. There's a corporation in Chicago I've worked with for several years now, and I've come to know a vice president there. Whenever I go in to visit the office, he's happy to sit and chat, and I never get the sense that he is short on time or passionately needing to tackle the next big thing on his list. For much of the year, he doesn't exude a sense of urgency, to my mind anyway. But then October rolls around, and this man becomes a powerhouse of energy, planning the huge event his organization is known for, one that attracts people from all over the world. He does a phenomenal job that month; he's just killing it while he pulls off quite an extravaganza. Even so, I think of him as a Jogger overall.

Sometimes it seems like Joggers absorb the energy around them, speeding up when surrounded by Runners and slowing down when surrounded by Walkers. This can make for some complicated dynamics in the workplace, and I'll go into that more in Part III.

Because Joggers need recognition and praise as their "fuel," they may feel some resentment toward the Runners in the organization, because Runners reap accolades without even trying. Runners can go at full speed and somehow make it look easy, and then they shrug off the praise and run some more—which is likely to drive a Jogger nuts. Do you remember the movie *Amadeus*, which won eight Academy Awards in 1985, including Best Picture? The story is told through the eyes of Antonio Salieri, the respected court composer for the Holy Roman Emperor during the late 1700s.

Salieri is secure in his position and confident of his musical talent—until Wolfgang Amadeus Mozart arrives in Vienna and effortlessly manages to show up Salieri with his considerable genius. Of course, Salieri feels threatened and resentful, even while he is in awe of Mozart's superior talent and achievement. This illustrates perfectly how a Jogger might feel when she is upstaged by a Runner over and over again.

The good news is, Joggers can play a strong supporting role to Runners. And there are ways to help a Jogger accelerate within your organization, as we'll see later in the book.

3

Walkers lack motivation

Wanda has been working on the bus for many years now, and she has the amount of effort it takes to get through the day down to a science. She knows exactly how long the route is and the best places to stop for a break. Most important, she knows precisely how to pace herself so she's not too tired at the end of the day—because, after all, her bowling team needs her to show up with pep in her step and ready to win every Tuesday and Thursday night. Wanda doesn't like change and, oh boy, she lets the driver know that when he announces an inconvenient detour. It makes her very nervous when Rufus starts spouting ideas and plans for so-called improvements. She also doesn't understand why Rufus and

Joan have to rush so much. After all, the route will get done
whether they dash through it or take their time. Slow and
steady, that's Wanda's motto!

It makes me sad to say that I have worked with many Walkers during my career.

These are the workers who do not contribute to any forward momentum at all. They plod and stumble and don't even keep up with the Joggers. They are practically being pulled along by the bus, with their legs draggin' as they trip over their feet. And they'll often wonder out loud, "Why are we going so fast? Why are you always making more work for yourselves?"

Walkers love to point out everything that they see is wrong in the organization; they do this because they want to deflect any blame that could be placed on them. They will talk negatively about the Runners and declare the reason that those individuals are going above and beyond is because they want attention. Sometimes they will complain to the bosses that the Runners are "making them look bad," and that they shouldn't be expected to do things that aren't in their job descriptions. They talk negatively about administration and spread bad energy. It's a toxic crisis.

I once taught with a teacher who complained constantly and would say things like:

"Hey, did you hear the principal is going to make us do extra carpool duties? Well, I bet extra breakfast duty is next. Doesn't that burn you up? She's treating us like slaves."

Or:

"Hey, did you notice that so-and-so came in at ten this morning? How did she pull that off without getting reprimanded? This place isn't fair. If you or I came in late, we'd hear about it. Doesn't that burn you up?"

The Walkers make comments like that *because they are trying to pull people down to their speed.* If everyone is moving slowly, it doesn't highlight that one individual isn't pulling her weight. And if everyone is united against the administration, there is safety in numbers, and the Walker isn't alone in the protest. Unfortunately, in education, ultimately it is the students who suffer when a school's faculty is made up of Walkers. An uninspired or negative teacher simply cannot motivate students to be their best selves or develop a lifelong love of learning. Within the public school system, the Walkers don't just let the organization down; they have a negative impact on our society as a whole, as their plodding pace essentially creates a "lost generation" of children who may never reach their full potential.

The Walker I mentioned above would latch on to new hires quickly. As soon as a new teacher came on board, she would bake her a Bundt cake and take her a share of some of her school supplies. She would say, "I know how hard it is to get started, and I want to be here for you." The new teachers would exclaim, "I just love her," but I grew to recognize that she was just trying to grow her "posse of poison."

Every day at lunch they would sit together in a huddle and whisper and gossip in hushed tones, and then they would all laugh. I said to myself, "She is ruining their lives." She was growing her negative group, because there is safety in numbers, and Walkers know that if they can get everyone to walk there will be no demands for them to move faster. I realized those in her group would grow to see negativity everywhere and that they'd take that home to their spouses. I saw them having fights at home and eventually getting divorced. I saw their own children resenting them and growing apart from them when they got older. I saw those teachers just getting old and sitting in rest homes all alone, bored and miserable. Yes, that's extreme, but isn't it the truth?

In the corporate world, new hires within the organization are often a favorite target of veteran Walkers. They will latch on to these new workers quickly. They will befriend them, pop by their cubicles with a lunch invitation, and offer to help them get adjusted in whatever way is needed. They will share "advice" with their new colleagues and take them out for a drink after work, and, quite honestly, they will seem to be wonderful colleagues. The problem with this, however, is that they are often trying to recruit new Walkers. They want to bond with the new hires so they can pull them in and form an alliance with them. Because, let's face it, the last thing a Walker wants is for a new hire to come in and outrun her. Walkers need the new hires to listen to them, to trust them, and to slow down to their level. They want to get more people to slow down, because then the bus goes slowly, and Walkers are content at that speed.

Don't trust the Bundt cake.

I have noticed that Walkers tend to be very focused on themselves. You will hear them wonder out loud why they were passed up for a promotion or why they were not chosen to attend a conference. They often feel picked on and will

claim that the work environment—specifically the favorit-
ism shown to Runners—is extremely unfair. I once sent five
Runners to a conference that was costly for the school. They,
however, had earned it and deserved it. A Walker said to me,
"I see the favorites are getting to go to the conference." I said,
"Excuse me," and she replied, "It's fine, Mr. Clark, it's just
that I didn't even know I had an option of going to the conference." To that, I replied, "You didn't." That afternoon in
the faculty meeting I explained that the "favorites," as she
called them, are the people who work hard and do their job
to the best of their abilities. The position of a favorite in life,
I explained, isn't chosen, it's earned, and anyone who has the
desire to reap the rewards of hard work can and should do so.

Well, I make it quite clear at RCA that it is my intent to
treat everyone fairly, but I am certainly not going to treat
everyone equally.

I make it a point to treat my Runners differently from
my Walkers, because as soon as the Runners realize they will
receive equal treatment no matter how hard they work, they
will begin to decelerate. There is nothing more frustrating
than to give 100 percent to a cause and see others who produce halfway work receiving the same pay, same bonuses,
same perks, and same treatment.

Take our education system, for example. Teachers are
paid based on how many years they have been in the system,
rather than having their salaries based on their performance.

Imagine what would happen if we ran our major corporations that way. Can you envision telling all of the corporate
executives that they will get paid the same amount, with
no hope for a promotion, as long as they hang around and
manage not to get fired? It's an antiquated concept, yet in
businesses across the country, corporations are rewarding
midlevel employees equally, regardless of their contributions
to the organization.

Here's how it works at RCA: If I receive funding for new
desks for a classroom, it goes to the Runners. If we have
money to get a class a set of computers, it goes to a Runner.
And when Walkers complain that they don't receive perks, or
not enough, I explain that rewards have a direct correlation
to performance. It may seem uncomfortable or harsh, but it's
necessary if you truly want to create an organization where
your bus is going to fly. If you don't operate in this manner,
your Runners will feel devalued and they will leave, and then
you will be left with a team of Walkers who are not only
barely moving your bus, but actually are driving your organization into the ground. You are supposed to be the Driver,
so don't let the Walkers take over your job, because they will
if you let them.

The good news is that Walkers (as well as Joggers) can
often improve under a system that rewards performance. In
chapter 15, you'll read about a teacher at RCA who started
out walking but is now running.

4

Riders are dead weight

Ridley arrives at the depot a few minutes late every morning, but that's okay, really, because everyone knows he's not a morning person, and they never leave without him anyway. Plus, he figures he is pretty much entitled to this job, so he's happy to let Rufus and Joan pick up his slack. Ridley no longer even pretends to pull the bus—except for, you know, when the boss man makes the rounds, but that doesn't happen more than once a day. The rest of the time, he has his feet up, his Starbucks cup in hand, and the morning paper spread out beside him. There's a paycheck at the end of the week and a nice retirement package just ten years down the line—sweet! Someone once told Ridley that he was slowing

down the whole bus, but he just can't see that. The bus is moving, people! Who cares where the momentum is coming from?!

One of the biggest challenges any organization can face is dealing with what I call the Riders. They are dead weight, because they have picked up their feet and are sitting there cross-legged! They say the bus stinks, and they don't like their seats. Regardless of what is happening, they choose to do nothing. So if there is a flat tire, they are going to watch others change it. If we need to get gas, they will watch others pump it. They contribute next to nothing to the organization, and they are literally just riding. What's worse is that they each feel 100 percent entitled to that seat.

Riders do not care about the overall success of the organization. In fact, they don't even care about their own personal success. They aren't trying to win awards or get recognition. They just exist. They can be a black hole of negative energy in an organization, a spot void of any positive growth or hope. They can often make the Runners and Joggers extremely frustrated, and they sometimes receive the most attention from leaders who are desperately trying to motivate them and fix the situation.

So why don't bosses just fire all the Riders? It may be because Riders are very adept at hiding in plain sight, particularly in the corporate world where it may be hard to keep tabs on legions of midlevel workers. It may also be due to a lack of performance metrics for certain types of jobs. If every department—even the mailroom—had such metrics, you could possibly get rid of the Riders. Another reason might be that some people don't seem relevant—like the mailroom clerk. But every person at every level has a contribution to make, so smart companies measure everything and everyone.

Think about a Rider who works in the position of switchboard operator at a very large corporation. He answers the phone, but he does it in an unhelpful manner that does nothing to enhance the company's image or uplift the customers who are calling. Is it worth your time to build a case to fire someone like that? Are you even aware of the true impact this Rider has on your organization or able to measure the average time he keeps callers on hold? Essentially, Riders do not want to lose their jobs or their paychecks, so their main goal is to do just enough that they can't be terminated.

In some cases, Riders will document how others are treated so they will have evidence to support their case in the event that they are fired. For example, if a Runner is reprimanded for wearing unprofessional attire, he will want to use that as a case of workplace unfairness if he notices others who wear similar attire without consequences. The Riders are the ones who are most apt to file a lawsuit, and being fired unfairly might actually make them happy, because they could potentially use that for a big payday.

In our public education system, it is notoriously difficult to fire a tenured teacher. If you do a simple Google search, you will find any number of news stories about teachers who kept their jobs even after they were found to be completely ineffective or to have done something unethical. In some cases, it was documented that the students slept or played video games in class while the teacher stood by and did nothing that resembled teaching. When a tenured teacher is a Rider, it is indeed a bad situation for everyone.

So what can be done to help Riders pick up their feet? In the next chapter, I'll explain why it may not even be worth your effort.

5

Drivers steer the organization

Drew has recently become the head Driver of this bus. His mission is to transform the bus into an amazing, turbo-charged machine that can leave the competition in the dust. To accomplish this, Drew knows he needs a stellar team of people who can not only supply the muscle power but can also brainstorm wonderful new ways to pick up speed. To-day, he's taking stock of the workers already assigned to the bus. Wow, that Rufus is a force to be reckoned with, but sometimes when he's going at the speed of light, he makes a serious mistake. Joan has some real potential, but Drew really wants to empower her to show a little more initia-tive. Wanda is very likable, but let's face it: she's plodding

*along like a turtle. What would motivate her to get going?
And Ridley is a disaster, plain and simple. What to do, what
to do?*

At the Ron Clark Academy, I'm the Driver of our bus. I have
developed my own philosophy for steering the organization,
and it goes something like this: I support the Runners first
and then, while they are off and running, I turn my attention to the Joggers, Walkers, and Riders either to help them
improve or to kick them off the bus.

Some of my early experiences in education have led me
to this philosophy, and I want to tell you an anecdote about
how I got there, so you can understand some key points.

Earlier in my career, I was working at a school where
there was a mix of Runners, Joggers, Walkers, and Riders.
One Rider in particular was just the worst! Each day she
would give the students worksheets while she sat at her desk
and read magazines. If the students made a sound, she would
yell at them, "Shut up!" She had a stool in the middle of her
room, and once or twice a day she'd drag herself to it and
plop upon the perch like a beanbag on a thimble and drone
on and on while the kids stared vapidly. I called it the "stool
of drool" because the students would literally put their heads
on their desks and begin to drool.

I honestly would lie awake in bed at night and think
about those poor children. I knew she was eradicating their

love of learning, and it bothered me to no end. I couldn't imagine why she wouldn't want to try her best to make an impact on the lives of her students, and I wondered if she had any clue how detrimental her behavior was to our school as a whole. During one of those sleepless nights, I essentially vowed to myself that I would turn this Rider into a Walker. And I did try. In fact, I put a great deal of effort into it. But the experience taught me how little value there is in trying to improve the Riders.

Here's what happened:

I bounced into this Rider's classroom early on Monday morning, mustered the happiest disposition possible, and asked if she'd be willing to coteach a lesson with me. Her eyes rolled around as I spoke of how fun it would be, and she scoffed, "It sounds like a lot of unnecessary work." I assured her I would do the lion's share and that it wouldn't be hard at all. She seemed to consider it, but then said, "No, I've got my system. This is the way I've always done things, and my system works."

With my hopes fading, I did the only thing I could think to do. I dug deep to muster sincerity, looked her right in the eyes, and said, "I need you. You are such a good math teacher, and I want to improve. I know there is a lot I could learn from you." It was as if the heavens opened. Her smile widened and, in the smuggest manner possible, she boasted, "Well, I do know my math. I guess I could help you out."

In the coming days, I tried to get her to help me, but she was so difficult that I really had to plan 98 percent of the lesson myself. When we cotaught her class, I noticed something. She was actually a very intelligent person, perhaps even the smartest in the school, but often it's the most intelligent workers who have trouble relating to others and using their abilities. They may know the content, but they aren't aware of how to transfer that knowledge to others. I watched her try to explain a math concept to the students, and even though the kids were clueless and clearly not getting it, she kept on steamrolling through without hesitation.

I realized a major point:

I don't care how smart you are, if you don't have a strong work ethic, then you are slowing down the bus.

When students asked questions, she would just seem frustrated by their lack of comprehension. When she talked above the kids' level of understanding, they would just stare at her, but she was oblivious to their confusion. Whenever I stopped her to clarify her points to the class, they would all go, "Ohhhh!" as they suddenly got it. She seemed shocked and would quickly add, "Yes, that is what I just said. That's exactly what I just said." The good news was that, when we cotaught my class, she described the math skills in the way I had done in her class. *Hmm, progress*, I thought.

The next day I said to her, "Hey, I noticed that other teachers are starting to decorate their doors. Maybe you should, too." She replied, "Oh, I'd just have to take it down before you know it." I smiled and told her, "Oh, I'll help you put it up, and I'll take it down. I just think it'd look great. What's your favorite color?" And it went on from there, and eventually I got that door decorated.

For weeks, I worked with that woman until finally, after a month, I stood back, and I realized I had her walking. Now, she wasn't jogging, and she damn sure wasn't running, but she was walking. I felt a great deal of pride at the improvement, but when I stepped back and looked at the entire school, I realized that nothing had really changed. Everything looked the same. Everything felt the same. I had gotten a Rider to walk, but that type of marginal improvement really wasn't going to change the speed of our bus. All of my energy, sleepless nights, and tireless efforts put into changing a Rider had, in essence, been a waste of my time. I'm telling you this so you don't make the same mistake in your organization. I don't want to spend my life getting Riders to walk. That's not my life's mission, and I doubt it is yours either. We all want the bus to *fly*, don't we? We want to inspire and achieve greatness and be part of something special! Picture the bus right now with the people in Fred Flintstone Position. Is getting the Rider to drop his legs and muster up the strength to start to walk really going to move the bus? Nope.

Getting a team of Runners to run long and hard with passion and energy is what moves the bus!

Keeping all of that in mind, and remembering the negligible effect my efforts had on the entire organization in that case, I decided to use a different tactic at RCA. As the administrator there, I decided to direct my attention to the Runners.

Now, in the business world we rarely focus on our Runners because they are doing a great job and, therefore, we think they don't require a lot of our attention. You can look a Runner in the eyes and give her fifteen seconds of sincere praise, and she will run for ten days straight. It takes so little fuel to fire them up, and they tend to do their job so well that they don't require a lot of directional guidance from leadership. But even so, I started to wonder if I was getting the most out of the Runners.

I started by asking the Runners if they needed help, and I gave them whatever resources I could find. They often acted shocked and were hesitant to accept my help, because another characteristic of Runners is that they tend to be overachievers and are used to doing everything themselves. They would respond, "No, no, I've got it," and I would have to insist that they allow me to help. But then they would agree, and they would exclaim, "Well, if you do this for me, I could go and take care of this other project I'm working on." And that made sense, because Runners are never done.

In their minds, there is always more to do, and they often feel like failures because they haven't accomplished enough. It's a battle that's impossible to win, however, because Runners always think there is more they should have done.

I started to find out what tasks they had on their plate, and, when I could, I would remove certain things that I knew others could do for them. I'd say, "Oh, I can get this taken care of for you," and as soon as you take something off the plate of a Runner, they will add something else back on. By helping to support their efforts, I was really freeing them up to be even more productive.

When the Runners did begin to take my help, however, I saw a shift. They seemed to have more energy and a renewed vision. When I praised their efforts and congratulated them publicly, they beamed, and when I found resources and other materials that they needed, they were shocked and grateful. For every ten minutes I spent on a Runner, the amount of effort they put forth grew exponentially. Sometimes I would just sit down with a Runner and talk about their ideas and give them words of encouragement, and they would become even more driven. After a month of trying this technique, I sat back and witnessed a school that was electric. You could practically feel the swell of passion in the halls, and I started to notice that the energy of the Runners was starting to rub off on the Joggers. The fire spread, and it spread from the top down.

It was then that I realized that we, as administrators, are often focusing our attention in the wrong areas. Instead of putting so much of our effort into rehabilitating our Riders, perhaps we should throw all we have to our Runners, for that is what truly moves the bus.

Having Runners maintain their speed is far more beneficial than having one Rider drop her feet and begin to walk.

After realizing how well the parable of the bus applied to our school environment, I was then able to explain it to the staff and express how much I value those who are Runners. I told the story of the bus, and I explained that we needed to be a school of Runners, and that our goals are far too important to walk or ride. I let the staff know that each of them may not necessarily want to run or jog, and I said that if that were the case, then that was okay because there were other buses they could get on. However, I made clear to them that on our bus, we were going to run!

As I began shifting my focus as an administrator, I began to learn more about how to deal with my Runners. That's when I really began to look at our organization like a bus and started to see how the different personalities fell in different categories.

Once I started to categorize my team members, I began to notice that my Runners, while awesome, tended to make many mistakes. I found myself having to deal with their mishaps more than anyone else's on the staff. I knew they were trying so hard to do a great job, and it amazed me how they could slip up so often.

One day, I sat down with one of my Runners, Mrs. Sanders, and explained to her that the mistakes were going to have to stop. I told her that she was one of my top Runners and that her errors were hurting the entire team. She dropped her head, apologized, and said it would not happen again. As she left my office, I felt sick. I knew I had hurt her, but I needed to make my point that the mistakes had to stop, didn't I? She was a Runner, and I expected more of her.

Over the next few days, I noticed how she would walk around the school with less pep and how she seemed to be so sad. She was carrying that conversation with me around with her, and when Runners are weighted down with the shame of their mistakes, they will never run as fast as they once did. It will weigh on them and hold them down. It will break their spirit.

And then, after some time, I realized something. The reason that my Runners, like Mrs. Sanders, were making the most mistakes is because they were doing a hundred different things. They were in charge of teams, leading projects, taking kids on field trips, dressing in costumes, creating phenomenal lessons, and uplifting the whole school. Their plates were full, and it made sense that if they were trying a hundred things that they were bound to mess up three of them.

On the other hand, my Riders were trying only two things and messing up three of them! I then learned that when my Runners made mistakes, I had to let it go. I had to overlook it and focus on the ninety-seven things they were doing well. I had to convince myself that it was perfectly okay and normal for them to mess up some things, and I realized that if I pointed out their errors too often, that it would kill their spirits.

I have also experienced firsthand what a Runner feels like when he makes a mistake. Several years ago, I meant to send an email to our staff about the learning difficulties and challenges we were having with a student at our school. I accidentally sent the email out to the entire school, meaning the *entire school*! It went to every parent of every student, and I was mortified. As emails started to pop in my box saying things like, "Mr. Clark, I think that was meant for just your staff," I thought I was going to vomit. One mom said, "Mr. Clark, I didn't read the information in the email, but I don't think it was meant for us." Now, she was one of the nosiest moms on Earth, and I knew good and well she'd read it! Not knowing what to do, I just got in my car and drove straight to the home of the child so that I could apologize to his mother. I said to myself, "She is going to spit in your face, and you are going to stand there and let her." When she opened the door, she was shocked and asked why I was there. I dropped my head, put my hands over my face, took a deep breath and said, "I've made a big mistake." She replied, "Mr. Clark, are you talking about that email? It's okay, everybody knows he's a little off." She was, of course, joking and trying to make light of the situation.

I said, "I think I should quit. I don't deserve to run a school after making a mistake like that."

And she replied, "Mr. Clark, you're being stupid. Maybe now everyone will see what we're dealing with and be able to help us."

She was so understanding, but I couldn't let it go. I would lie in bed and think about it and wonder if every parent in the school was concerned I was going to blast their child's business all over the place.

After that, whenever I would sit down to email people, I would remember my error, and my heart would sink. I made careful effort to ensure I was emailing only the correct individuals each time. I just couldn't let it go. In some ways, it broke some of my spirit. And then, one day I was walking down the second floor hallway of our school, and I had a realization. I said to myself, "You're a Runner. It's okay for you to make mistakes, too! Get over it!" And I let it go. Seriously, I brushed it off and moved on, because I realized that I wouldn't be able to run as fast if I carried that mistake.

Dear Runners, it is okay to allow yourself to make a mistake. Give yourself permission to forgive yourself and move on. You can't run with a mistake on your heart. Let it go.

And remember this important lesson:

As an administrator, there is nothing you can do that is more detrimental to the organization than kill the spirit of your Runners.

I also had to learn to say yes to my Runners.

Runners always have new ideas, and when they would bring them to me, I would often say no, because I felt the idea wouldn't work or that it would call for too much effort or resources. I had to learn, however, that sometimes, even though I didn't necessarily agree with the idea, I had to give it my approval in order to keep the spirit of my Runners intact.

We were hosting a national educators' conference at RCA, and my staff came to me with an idea for all of us to dress in white suits. They said we would look incredible and that all of the visitors could easily identify us as RCA staff. Well, I just don't wear all white like that. It was the dead of winter, and as pale as I was, it was going to completely wash me out, and I knew I would look like a ghost. But the people asking me were my Runners, so I replied, "Sure, let's do it." The opening night of the national conference, we were about to open the doors to let everyone in, and I looked over at my team. They were cheering, jumping up and down, and taking pictures of each other. They were dressed in all white, psyched, and on fire! And that is the type of energy you get when your Runners are fueled.

And what I have seen is that, by making support for the Runners the foundation of how I lead, we have created a climate and culture at our Academy that is positive and re-freshing. Those who work hard are recognized for it; they are respected and uplifted. It is a heaven for those who wish to run, and it is for that reason that our organization has been able to accomplish so much.

Our bus flies.

And yours can too!

PART II

How to Accelerate

After a speech I made in Oklahoma City, a lady walked up to me with tears in her eyes. She leaned in to me and said, "I'm a Walker, but I want to run." It broke my heart, and I realized that within all of us there is a desire to be better. We have something within us that leads us to want to contribute to something bigger than ourselves.

Are you a Runner? Do you want to be? No matter how fast you're currently moving, I believe unequivocally that the desire to run is within us all.

At previous jobs where I was surrounded by Riders and Walkers, I felt defeated and lost. It was clear to me that there was no way I could move that entire bus on my own. Yet I realized that regardless of how bad my surroundings were, I could make an impact. If the bus didn't move fast, maybe I could decorate the bus and make it livable. Maybe I could roll down the windows so that it wouldn't be so hot. Maybe I could spray some air freshener.

Even if everyone around you, including the boss, is in crisis, you can still contribute and make things better. There is always something that you can do. There is always a way to accelerate, regardless of your co-passengers.

So how can you be better? What can you do? If you have never run a marathon, you probably shouldn't go out and enter one tomorrow. And if you have never "run" at work, then you probably won't go from zero to sixty overnight either. It happens in stages, because it is a process.

At our school, we make this statement to our students at the beginning of each year:

You can spend your time at our school however you choose, but you can only spend it once.

The same goes for this year in your organization. You can only live it once, so why not make it the year you choose to run!

If you want to accelerate, start here. This section will describe the habits and behaviors that many Runners have in common. It will empower you with important new insights that can help you succeed. It is a road map for your journey.

Along the way, you'll become better acquainted with the characters we met in the last section and have a chance to observe their exploits in pulling the bus. If you're having trouble recalling their names, here they are, one more time.

Cast of Characters

Rufus... The **R**unner

Joan... The **Jo**gger

Wanda.. The **Wa**lker

Ridley .... The **Ri**der

Drew... The **Dr**iver

6

Get there early

The sun is rising on the bus depot, and Drew, the Driver, arrives to find a crisis situation: four flat tires. Yikes! His strongest performer, Rufus, is away at a conference, so Drew knows he'll have to tackle this calamity on his own. He rolls up his sleeves, gets out the jack, and then he hears, "Let me help you with that." It's Joan, arriving early, as she so often does, and she is ready and willing to pitch in. Drew is flooded with relief and immense gratitude. Joan may not be the fastest Runner on his team, or even the most adept at changing tires, but just the fact that she is there makes Drew feel indebted to her. Just by arriving early, Joan became the

most valuable player on the team that day. By the time the others show up at 9:00 sharp, the crisis is solved and the day can begin. Whew!

When you are consistently at least a few minutes early to arrive at work and to meetings, you give your boss great peace of mind, and that elevates your status on the bus.

If you aren't quite running at your job, then the last thing you want to do is to get in the way of those who are. Whenever there is a group meeting, you want to make sure you are among the first people there, because the Runners are almost always going to be early. You certainly don't want to show up late, because they may have to wait for your arrival, and not only does that show that you don't respect the purpose of the meeting, but it also shows that you don't respect your colleagues' time. A Runner's time is valuable, and you don't want to be the cause of wasting any of it.

At RCA, we always start our staff meetings promptly at 4:05 p.m., and we have expressed the importance of being on time repeatedly. The problem is, we dismiss an entire school filled with students at four, so there are always last-minute issues to deal with that will sometimes cause people to be a few minutes late. We have asked our staff that if something happens that keeps them a minute or two late, the second they walk into the staff meeting, they should be obviously moving quickly and that they should apologize to the group as they walk in, even if it interrupts the meeting. It works for us.

We used to have an employee who somehow managed to come in late to every meeting. Even after I had met with him and asked him to be on time or at least appear as if he were trying to get to the meeting quickly, he still entered the room so slowly, as if to let everyone know that he didn't mind that he was late and he wasn't about to walk quickly. It unnerved me to no end. Needless to say, he is no longer with RCA. I think he was trying to make a point that he wasn't going to be made to hurry, but what he didn't realize was that he was upsetting the entire team, because he didn't value their time. It made him look foolish.

I am often astounded when I hear friends who work in the corporate world talk about the way people trickle in to meetings fifteen or even thirty minutes late. If you know the meeting won't start until a quarter hour past the appointed time, you may be tempted to start showing up fifteen minutes late yourself, so you don't waste that time just sitting around waiting. Don't do it. Don't become one of those people who are stealing valuable minutes from other team members. Instead, do your part to promote a culture of integrity and dependability. Show up to meetings a few minutes early, even if you have to bring work with you so you're not sitting idle.

At RCA we have a different staff member do breakfast duty each morning at 7:10. There are some staff members who have never been late, not once. On the days they are scheduled, I rest easy, and that's a great feeling. There are others whose performance is spotty, and when they have breakfast duty, I have a pit in my stomach worrying that they might not be there—even if they ultimately arrive on time. Even if the person has been on time four out of every five times, it's that fifth time that gives me pause. You may think that since you were late just once or twice that it's not a big deal, but it is the *doubt* in your performance that you put in the mind of your leader that causes the greater problem.

Now, let's say you just are not a morning person and that you can't get up any earlier. You manage to make it to work on time, but you simply can't get there any earlier. Well, you have an obligation then to stay on past the time you were supposed to leave. You need to show that your work ethic is sound and that you are willing to put in the time to perform at a high level. After I made that point to a member of our team, I was happy to see that he was staying later each day. But when I went into his office to thank him, I saw that he was on Facebook. It ruined the moment. When I am saying stay later, what I am really saying is "work later." Even if you can stay only thirty minutes past quitting time, do it. Remember: you want to be part of something great, and this is a small way to contribute to the greater whole.

While it's obvious that school has to start on time, punctuality is a little less straightforward in the business world these days because so many corporations have flextime. Even so, whether you realize it or not, everyone you work with knows if you are consistently cutting your days short. It's one of those things that everyone notices, even though no one ever mentions it. People want to know what the expectations are of everyone, so they are looking to see what everyone else is doing. They notice when your car is in the parking lot, and whether the lights in your office are on or off, and how long you stay gone for lunch. This is just something you can't escape; it's public knowledge.

Over time, when you develop a reputation for always being early and ready to hit the ground running when you arrive, you earn great respect. Your boss may never point out how wonderful it is that you are always there, but it increases your worth in her mind.

7

Wear your good clothes

Rufus is all pumped up. Drew called for a day of staff meetings and arranged for a nice lunch to be delivered. Because Rufus plans on pitching a wide assortment of ideas, he dresses carefully in a suit and tie—a red tie, because that communicates confidence. He usually has to dress a bit more casually to pull the bus, so it's fun to put on his "boardroom clothes" today. At the meeting, ideas start to fly as Rufus notes with approval that Joan has also chosen an especially smart outfit—and shoes with a heel! Then Ridley, who is dressed in a sloppy shirt with no tie, drops a bomb, an idea so breathtakingly dim-witted and obtuse that Rufus can't even process it. Every bit of energy, goodness, and light van-

ishes from the room. Okay, okay, maybe it wasn't that bad.
But it's pretty much a given that ideas from people who dress
down sound bad, and Ridley looks like a slob today.

I don't think people realize that everything you say or do is
always better when you have on sharp attire. When you are
in a meeting and you give an idea, it seems smarter and more
logical when you are neat, professional, and dressed to kill.
At our school, it is the expectation that everyone wears suits
and business attire every day.

There are no dress-down days, because our performance is
never dressed down.

I have even asked our basketball coaches to show up for
games wearing a tie, despite the fact that the coaches for all
the other teams are in sweatpants or jeans and a sweatshirt.
That's just how we do things at RCA.

If you happen to work for a company that has a looser re-
quirement in terms of attire, like a technology firm perhaps,
you still want to make sure that you dress better than the expectation. And if your firm mandates a dress code like "smart
casual" or "business casual," you want to be sure you know exactly what that means—especially if you're starting a new job
with a new company and will be shopping for a new wardrobe.

It isn't always about the clothing; it's often about how you wear it. You want to appear pulled together and well groomed. If you shake hands with people throughout the day, consider getting a manicure every two weeks. If you wear a tie to work, make sure that the bottom of it falls precisely at the midpoint of your belt buckle. Don't come to work with your hair still wet or in a skirt whose length screams "spring break." Just because others dress down doesn't mean you should, too. In other words, take pride in your appearance. You want your attire to improve the look and feel of the space.

Don't allow your work ethic to "run" while your outfit rides.

You and your attire should both run, because, if you want to run, you need to look the part. If you want to earn respect, know that it comes from not only how you perform but also how you look while doing it.

In the same vein, the neatness of your environment means a lot to those around you. You may be completely fine with piles of papers on your desk, pictures taped to the wall, and piles of clutter, but keeping your space clean is also about contributing to a successful environment. At RCA, I make a point to pick up even the tiniest bits of paper or trash from the floor, and by doing so, our staff and student body have learned that the expectation is to keep our school spotless. Not ignoring the smallest items ensures that everyone realizes that anything larger simply wouldn't be tolerated. It's all about respect of the environment and the people in it. You may be fine with your work space being disheveled, but others aren't. You're bothering them even if they never mention it. For the sake of the organization as a whole, keep it clean. No one wants to ride on a messy bus!

8

Say hello

Drew has the bus idling in the depot; he's jotting down notes for a memo while he waits for his team to arrive. Rufus arrives early, cheerful and smiling, and looks Drew in the eye while he says "Good morning!" and asks about the day's itinerary. Joan is next to arrive; her greeting is also cheery. Wanda merely nods at Drew and makes a beeline for the coffeepot. Ridley, who is actually on time for a change, boards the bus last. He is too busy texting to even look. Some people are like that. Quite often, they trip and fall flat on their faces.

I am astonished by the number of people in workplace environments who don't even greet one another. Let people know you *see* them and acknowledge them with a smile.

Before the beginning of every school year, I stand before my staff and tell them that of everything they will do that year, from teaching amazing lessons to developing parent relations to inspiring students, that there is one thing that will make me more proud of them than anything else. That simple act is to uplift one another. I explain that if we stand strong as a unit, then everything else will fall into place. And that can start simply, with a kind greeting. Whether it's in the hall, on the elevator, or at the start of a meeting, look people straight in the eyes, smile, and say, "Good morning." You may not be doing the heavy lifting and running at work, but the least you can do is be cheerful and lift up those who may be doing more. And if you spread good energy, good energy will come back to you!

Now RCA is small enough that the faculty and staff all know one another. But at very large corporations, this is not the case. You may know everyone in your own department, but run into strangers a dozen times a day in the elevator, the corridor, or the cafeteria. In a business environment, a greeting may be even more than a way to acknowledge and uplift people—it may be a valuable means of networking within your workplace, particularly if you hope to make a lateral move into another department that is more appealing to you. You could not only say hello, but also introduce yourself and find out a little bit about the other person. It's a great way to learn names, build relationships, and become more visible within your organization. It might open doors that allow you to work on special projects, like serving on a diversity council or helping to organize the annual holiday party or a community service event. Once you start meeting people, always follow up with them, whether it's by asking them out for coffee or connecting with them on LinkedIn. You may even find a mentor, a coach, or a sponsor who can help boost your career.

9

Sit with the Runners

Every morning, Ridley shuffles down the aisle, Starbucks cup in hand, with his eye on his favorite spot—that long bench-like seat at the very back of the bus. It's quiet, it's cozy, and he can stretch out for forty winks when the driver is occupied and busy. As far as Ridley is concerned, it's the best seat in the house. Today, Joan is waiting impatiently for him to move along and get out of her way, because she has her own seating strategy. She really wants to get a seat next to Rufus, before anyone else does. Rufus is fun to be around, and he's energetic and helpful. The day goes faster for Joan when she's working next to Rufus, and she does some of her best work

in his company. Everyone needs a muse. Or a mentor. Or maybe both, all rolled up into one.

I don't think I'll ever forget the movie *Mean Girls*. The main character, played by Lindsay Lohan, is a sweet, down-to-earth girl named Cady who starts out with a clean slate at a brand-new high school. Soon she meets three beautiful, popular classmates who also happen to be crude, vengeful, and just plain mean. The more Cady interacts with them, the more she becomes just like them—another mean girl.

This is what tends to happen in high school: you're inclined to acquire the characteristics of the people you choose to sit with, eat lunch with, and hang around with after school.

Guess what? This is a universal truth in life and in business as well—so you should give careful consideration to who you sit with. You may not have a seat in the boardroom or on a prestigious committee, but you can often find an opportunity to connect with those who are.

I work in education, yet I have always found ways to "sit with" influential leaders in the business community. Back in 2007, I applied for and was accepted into Leadership Atlanta, a leadership development program that aims to build a better community in Atlanta by fostering collaboration and including all perspectives in local decision-making initiatives. One day, everyone in that year's program was invited to participate in a bus tour around the city that would familiarize us with certain issues our community was facing. You better believe that before I got on that bus I carefully went over everyone else's bio, trying to decide whom I should try to sit next to and whom I must talk to. Maybe it's the teacher in me, but I made flash cards because I wanted to know not only where everyone worked but how many children they had and anything else that could prepare me to have a conversation with them. I knew that these were the people I needed to be around, and I wanted to be fully prepared to make the most of this opportunity. You can find similar opportunities in your community and ways to make the most of them. Coincidentally, eight of the high-powered individuals on that bus would later become board members at my school. Trust me, that wasn't by accident.

Recently I met with an RCA alumnus, a dynamic and talented young man who achieved great things at our school and who is now a Gates Millennium Scholar at the University of North Carolina. He had earned an internship at a prominent corporation in Atlanta, and I went to visit him there. As we sat in the break room, Osei was telling me how, just the day before, the CEO had actually come into the break room while he was there. So here was this kid, a freshman in college, sitting in a room with the chief executive officer of one of the most iconic corporations in the world.

He had a chance to speak with this very influential person, an opening to say hello and trade a few words, maybe make a lasting impression—and he didn't say anything at all. He said to me, "Mr. Clark, I wanted to go for it, but I just didn't want to bother him." And I can see how that could happen, how it might be easy to think *Oh, I shouldn't bother him or interrupt him*—but it was still a missed opportunity. That was a moment to shine, and you can't let those moments pass because you aren't willing to step up and speak to someone.

So, if you want a promotion, or to move forward, or to become more visible within an organization, you need to find ways to connect with the people who are already there. Say hello, be engaging, and let people know you are there!

10

Ask for help

Rufus had always been a B student in science. He had a lot of talents and he was good at a lot of things, but science just wasn't at the top of the list. Still, he was known for his groundbreaking ideas about how to make the bus go faster, and sometimes that meant he had to push himself to find practical applications for his spotty knowledge of energy, force, and matter. One day he thought he had it—a way to move the bus at the speed of sound. Instead, the bus tipped over and rolled down an embankment, coming to rest gently at the edge of a creek. "Why didn't you ask for advice?!" cried Drew, when he found out what had happened. "I used

to be a stunt driver. I easily could have told you how to com-
pensate for destabilizing forces!"

One year we had two brand-new teachers at RCA, and early in the fall each found himself in a sticky situation with a student's parent, a situation they were unsure how to handle in the best possible way. One of them decided to tackle the problem on his own; he went ahead, wrote an email, and sent it to the parent. And it was a disaster. It didn't go over well at all, the contents of that email. The other teacher came to me and asked, "How would you suggest I handle this situation?" And I replied, "I'm so glad you asked me. Here's what I would prefer you to do." The situation ended beautifully.

Don't be afraid to ask for direction when you need it. I think sometimes employees fall into this trap of thinking they must prove themselves by demonstrating they have all the answers—and that translates into being afraid to ask for help, even when they don't know what to do next.

I once had an assistant who was well intentioned but kept falling short of my expectations. I would give him a list of tasks, and he would go off to do them, and then he would come back to our next meeting with only half of that list done. What was up with the other half? Invariably, I would find out that he didn't know how to accomplish those tasks.

He'd run into a situation where I told him to go somewhere to get something and then it wasn't there. So instead of texting me and asking me where to look next, what to do next, he did nothing. He wouldn't communicate with me when he ran into a roadblock because he didn't want to show that he didn't know something.

Sometimes it's great to ask for direction, for help, or for clarity. It's not seen as a weakness. Instead, it makes it clear that you care enough about a project or a task to be sure you get it right. It's okay to ask for an explanation or to simply say, "I need clarification about what this means" or even "Could you give me a clear idea of the outcomes you expect?"

You can also ask for help in advancing within your organization. Tell your boss you want to do better and ask for specific suggestions. If your company has a formal mentoring program, I would encourage you to sign up so that you can be paired with a mentor who can give you ongoing advice and encouragement.

11

Accept criticism

As usual, Rufus is going at top speed, setting an inspirational pace for the others, and the team seems to be humming with his positive energy. And then—oops and double oops!— Rufus reaches for his sunglasses and, in doing so, he misses a turn. It's a really thoughtless error, and Drew has to focus his full attention on correcting the problem. Afterward, Drew gives Rufus a couple of quick pointers so they can avoid a similar problem in the future. "I am so sorry," says Rufus sincerely. "It will never happen again." Drew is grateful for that response. Last week, when he gave Wanda a simple suggestion, she became hostile and defensive—and the incident gave him nightmares in which Wanda became a huge hiss-

ing serpent that tried to squeeze the life out of him. There's nothing like waking up screaming to ruin a good night's sleep.

If you want to improve constantly, then you must tinker with the bus on a consistent basis. There are always ways to be more efficient and effective, and when the members of the team feel that their speed and their methods are sufficient and don't need to change, that is a mentality that stands in the way of progress.

As a leader, I am always suggesting ways that individuals on our team could have done things in a better or more effective way. When I point something out to the Runners, they are appreciative and accept the ideas with no hesitation. They will say, "Oh good idea, I'll remember that for next time," or "Very good idea. Got it!" If I have to point out something they did that was wrong, they'll say, "Oh, so sorry; it won't happen again," or "I'll fix it right now!" I love those types of responses, because the conversation is over, the point was made and accepted, and the bus can continue to run.

In other cases, giving constructive criticism to others doesn't go over so well. The generation between twenty-four and thirty-five years of age seems so shocked whenever someone points out something they did incorrectly, and they can become really defensive. We have built the young generation up in America as being so smart and gifted and special that they take offense when someone points out that something they did wasn't good enough. Their favorite reaction is, "Well, in my defense . . ." Or they'll say, "No one told me I was supposed to do it a different way."

I was working with a teacher who was having issues with three boys in her class. She wanted to write them up every day and send them to the office, so I finally sat down and suggested that she try to develop a better relationship with the boys. I told her that they weren't causing problems in any of their other classes, and that the other teachers had spent time trying to bond with the young men. I told her that it had worked for the others, so maybe it would work for her as well. And you would think I had slapped her.

She blew up at me and said, "Oh, so you are saying it's my fault?" I was taken aback and said, "No, I wasn't saying it's your fault; I was just offering a suggestion to fix the problem," and she responded, "No, you're saying I need to work harder to be kind to the boys and spend time with them so that they won't misbehave. You are making me feel like I have done something to make those boys be disrespectful, and it isn't my responsibility to fix it when it isn't my fault in the first place."

No matter what I said to her or no matter how I tried to explain, she wasn't willing to listen to me. She was completely missing the boat. The situation took a lot of time to resolve, and when that happens, the bus isn't running. We had to pull over to the side of the road and do some major mending, and that keeps progress from happening.

No matter where you work, if your boss comes to you and offers a suggestion for improvement, or if he has to point out something that you have done that is wrong, there is a magical way you can respond. It's nine simple words that will sound like heaven to your supervisor, and I learned them the hard way . . .

It was my first year teaching, and I handled a situation with a parent horribly. I had baked cookies for my students, but I didn't give any to the kids who didn't deserve a reward. In typical American parent fashion, a mother called me to complain that her daughter didn't receive a cookie and that she felt it wasn't fair and that I had ruined her daughter's self-esteem. I told her that her daughter wasn't working hard enough to earn a cookie. This mother quickly let me know that if I wasn't going to make enough cookies so that every child could have one that I shouldn't be making cookies. I responded, "I had plenty of cookies," and then jokingly added, "In fact, I think I ate your daughter's cookie." Not surprisingly, my joke didn't go over well, and she hung up on me.

The next morning I was called to the office. That mom was in there fussing and screaming at the principal, and to my best recollection, it was like the exorcist was in there.

Her head was spinning and there was green vomit all over the walls. The principal asked me to sit down, and after listening to the mother yell about how disrespectful I was, the principal looked the mom right in the eyes and said, "Mr. Clark made those cookies. If he didn't feel like your daughter has worked hard enough to deserve one of them, then I am going to support his decision."

The heavens parted. The mother was irate as she stormed out and slammed the door, and there I sat, in the presence of an administrator who actually "gets it" and who had my back. I loved her. And then, she leaned in to me and screeched. She said, "Mr. Clark, *what are you thinking?* Do you think this is how I want to start my day? You know that woman is like fire, so why are you going to add gasoline to it? Have you lost your mind? Are you crazy? You can't tell people you ate their daughter's cookie! What were you thinking?"

Honestly, the whole situation had me rattled. There were already tears in my eyes. I wanted to defend myself and explain how I shouldn't have to be nice to a parent who is rude to me and how I felt like I did nothing wrong. I didn't deserve being fussed at! I was in the right!

That is how I felt at age twenty-four. I, just like other twenty-four-year-olds, felt I could do no wrong. I was stubborn and didn't even know that there were things I didn't know. I thought I knew it all. I realize now that there are some things you can "see" only with age, and the sad thing is that if I tried to explain that to my twenty-four-year-old self, he wouldn't have believed me. He would have said, "Oh I get it," but he would have been clueless.

To all of you twenty-four- to thirty-five-year-olds: *You don't "see" yet. It's a gift that comes later, and the best advice I can give you is to trust us. We are older, and we may not quite have your energy, but we have our own super power, and it's an understanding of the world that you can't get at such young years. We have the power to "see beyond" what is before us and truly understand the dynamics and motivations that go into the actions around us. It's a wisdom that has to marinate over time, and when it comes, you will "see" situations much differently. There are some young adults reading this right now who are thinking, "Oh, I know what he means." You don't. You can't. Intellect does not afford you this superpower; it is only acquired with age.*

While I had wanted to defend myself when my principal was fussing at me, I was also scared and shocked. She had been so nice when the parent was in there, and I just didn't know how to handle it. I simply mumbled the only nine words I could get out of my mouth:

"I am so sorry. It will never happen again."

Instantly, the blood receded from the face of my principal. Her muscles relaxed, and she eased in her seat. She stopped yelling, and her eyes softened as she said, "Okay, Mr. Clark, go on back to your class and your cookies."

My eyes widened as I said, "Huh?"

Again, with a smile she gently said, "It's okay, go on back to your class and your cookies."

As I walked out of her office, I thought to myself, *Definitely bipolar.*

I honestly had no idea what caused the switch in her behavior, but years later, I get it, completely. As an administrator, I can tell you that when someone does something wrong, I simply want to point it out and have the person "hear it" and understand it so we can move on. I don't want to have a long discussion or hear the person's defense. I just want to know it won't happen again, because then the bus can keep moving and gain speed.

Trust me, you don't want to have the mentality that you're always right and you know everything. It's important to realize that your vision of the world isn't always as accurate as you may think it is, so you should be humble, open to suggestions, and willing to take criticism.

12

Clean the windshield

The team has been pulling the bus at top speed all morning and, inevitably, the windshield is now covered with bug splatter. There's nothing to do but stop, because, frankly, you can't run if you can't see the road in front of you. As they pull over to the side of the road, Rufus automatically starts to get out. "It's okay, I'll get it," says Joan quickly. She has noticed how much effort Rufus has put in this morning and she wants to support him the best she can—even if that means volunteering for a somewhat menial task. Wanda slumps down in her seat. She's not about to work the Windex bottle and the squeegee, because that has never been listed in her job description. Nope, NEVER.

When you're on a long road trip with friends, if you aren't the one driving, you need to do your part to contribute. You need to help navigate, remain awake and engage the driver in conversation, offer to pay for the gas, and, when you stop for a break, clean the dead bugs off the windshield. When someone else is doing the hard work, you want to support that person in this way, so she can focus on the road ahead and see it clearly.

That same logic applies at any workplace. If you aren't a Runner and you know you are not a Runner, you should volunteer to do the menial tasks, because the last thing the organization wants is for the Runners to have to waste their time on the mindless details.

When teachers first come to our school, they are like deer in the headlights. There's a lot to learn and a lot going on, and it's nearly impossible to start out as a Runner because you are just trying your best to keep up. I know it's the same for many people in the corporate world, particularly if they've changed jobs or industries or have assumed a new role within the same company or industry. It can be overwhelming just to figure out where to find the simplest of answers. When everything is new and foreign, it can take you twice as long as usual to do things you used to knock out quickly at your last job.

Of course, it's going to take you a while to get up to speed and hit your stride. But there are ways you can maximize your contribution while you're adjusting to your new position on the bus—and one of those ways is to clean the windshield.

In her first year at RCA, one of our new teachers was trying to take everything in, and it was obvious that she wasn't contributing as much to the school as the veterans were. Her lessons weren't as dynamic, she wasn't at a point where visiting educators could observe her teaching, and she didn't have a workshop to share with the visitors either. She wasn't in charge of any major programs, and honestly, she was just doing a basic job. She was walking. But she wanted to run!

I quickly noticed that whenever we needed someone to volunteer for something, she was the first to offer to help. She would set up tables, sweep floors, sell merchandise, cover classes, take on extra after-school duties, and jump in wherever she could. During a staff meeting, we announced that we needed someone to start taking the minutes of each meeting and then typing them out and sending to all members of the staff. Yuck, right?

Well, three Runners instantly raised their hand in typical Runner fashion. As I went to pick one, the new teacher spoke up and said, "No, I got it. I'll take the minutes." And in that instant, she earned an enormous amount of respect in my eyes. She realized that the Runners had enough on their plates, and she volunteered to do one of the worst tasks possible. That is the sacrifice we need those who aren't running to make for the organization.

Now, years later, that teacher is being observed by visiting educators, doing workshops, and contributing to our organization. But that didn't happen overnight. She started off by jumping in and taking on whatever she could, and, in doing so, she made it easier for the Runners to do their jobs. She didn't start as a Runner, but by saving the Runners time, she enabled the bus to soar.

At one of our staff meetings, I was sitting with the entire team, the new along with the veterans, and we were discussing a huge surprise project we wanted to do for the students. Then someone stepped into the room to let us know that a staff member was needed at carpool. We were all in the heat of planning, and I knew that no one wanted to leave, but I was hoping one of our new teachers who wasn't contributing as much would have jumped up and volunteered. Instead, the only one who stood up was Mr. King, one of our fastest Runners and best minds at RCA. He piped up, "I've got it," and before I knew it, he was out that door! But . . . I needed him in that meeting. Some of the others who stayed weren't the ones who were going to contribute the best ideas, but even more important, they weren't the ones who were going to do all of the work to pull off the project. Mr. King is instrumental to all we do, and I wished those who weren't the Runners at RCA would have realized that and stepped up to volunteer.

If you aren't going to be a Runner, at least you can take the menial tasks away from the Runners. By saving them from one hour of menial work, you are contributing a substantial degree of speed to the organization and doing a great service that does not go unrecognized. And if you're acting as a Driver, you can actively designate a Walker to get out and do the grunt work, so your top performers can continue to run at top speed.

13

Take the hint

Wanda had been noticing how well the new Driver, Drew, seemed to respond to the suggestions that Rufus and Joan were always making. He was always saying yes to them. Maybe Drew is a pushover, *she thought. Now, Wanda has no interest in making a suggestion that would create more work for any of them, but she has a wonderful idea for an oh-so-minor route change that would allow them to stop for lunch at her favorite barbecue spot. Pulled pork with mango salsa—YUM! Drew listens attentively to Wanda's suggestion, then politely explains to her that this idea just wouldn't work.* "No, really," *Wanda insists,* "it'll be great!" *She continues to push. And push. And push some more . . . until fi-*

nally Drew just has to shut her down. Wanda sulks the rest
of the day, and it really isn't pretty.

You have to know when and how to pick your battles. If
you are sitting in a meeting with your team and you make
a suggestion, it's important to read the temperature of your
supervisor—and be perceptive enough to realize that going
against the direction she is trying to go in will be very risky.

At RCA, we plan one day a year where we surprise the
students by telling them it is the "Best Day of School Ever!"
As soon as they arrive, we completely shock them by load-
ing them onto buses and taking them all over Atlanta, where
each of their classes takes place for one hour before they are
bussed to the next location. They may have science in a cage
with elephants at the zoo and then go to math class in Phil-
ips Arena, where they have to figure out the fastest way to
count the thousands of seats that are there. It's a great deal
of fun!

The first year we tried this at RCA, one of our staff members wanted to have the students participate in an activity
that would be very high energy and require a lot of movement. At the meeting with the team, I explained that we
didn't want to do that because our students would be in dress
uniforms and they'd get too sweaty. She replied that she'd already called the location and they said yes and that she really wanted to do it. I explained that the activity didn't even

tie in well with her academic subject and that she needed to find an activity that related to what she was teaching. She was visibly upset.

That night I got an email from her stating that she wanted me to reconsider letting her do the activity. I wrote back and again expressed that I didn't want the students to get sweaty in their dress uniforms and that she needed to find something else. The next day she came up to me and said, "Mr. Clark, I just wanted to talk to you one more time about my activity. I think it will be awesome if we could do it, because I can find a way to tie it in." I said, "Okay, go ahead and do it." I was obviously not happy about it, but she didn't even read my mood. She ended up doing that activity, but the kids did get sweaty, exhausted, and disheveled, and it wasn't what was best for that day. She got her way, and I'm sure she was happy about that, but her unwillingness to take my advice obviously stayed on my mind.

On the flip side, when another staff member presented an idea, I said I wasn't sure if it would work. She responded, "No problem, I have two other backup options!" She presented them both, and either one would have worked well.

In any business, in any industry, you must always learn how to read the person you answer to. It may be your supervisor, or it may be your clients. I have a friend who owns a graphic design firm, where he designs printed materials for large corporations as well as small businesses. When a client feels that a certain color scheme is too bright or a new logo design doesn't adequately communicate how dynamic her company is, the designer has to listen and respond appropriately. It doesn't matter what his own favorite colors are or how much he loves the new logo he came up with. If he cannot gauge the client's values and preferences—and then deliver on them—he risks losing out on repeat business. Over time, he can even develop a sort of sixth sense about the type of design, whether contemporary or classic, that each of his clients will respond to most favorably. And this is probably the best way to "take the hint"—to act intuitively, based on the totality of every hint that the person you answer to has ever dropped.

14

Listen more than you talk

Joan has just witnessed a conflict between Wanda and Drew, the Driver. Wanda was waving her hand around frantically in a meeting, wanting to be called on—and then threw out a bizarre and arbitrary route change and went on and on and on, explaining the dubious benefits of her suggestion and completely not hearing Drew when he said that it just wouldn't work. It was dawning on Joan just how different this interaction is from the discussions that take place between Rufus and Drew. Rufus says a lot less, but the Driver respects his opinions a lot more. Hmm, *thinks Joan,* maybe there's a lesson in this. *She decides she'll keep her hand down during meetings for a little while and listen to others*

instead. And she wishes Wanda would learn to sit *on her hands.*

When you meet with other team members, it's important to be present. You want to make eye contact with the speaker and look interested. Don't be on your computer or glancing at your phone. Don't do things that could distract others such as eating during the meeting or opening a candy wrapper. While it may not bother some, it will unnerve others. If you want to contribute to the group, and you don't really have the best ideas or you aren't willing to volunteer to take on the project, the least you can do is to be attentive and not interrupt the flow around you.

Another way to be attentive when you go to a meeting is to have a notepad. It is a sign of respect because it's your way of saying that you value what the person is about to tell you. If you are meeting with your colleagues and don't have a notepad and pen, you're saying you don't expect to take any initiative on what needs to be done. You're basically just an observer. Some will say that it's fine to bypass the notepad if you are going to type notes into a phone or other device. To cover your bases, bring both. It shows initiative.

And if you are riding or walking, the best advice I can give you about meeting conduct is to put your hand down. To be more specific, I'm saying do not raise your hand to share ideas or to criticize others' ideas—I'm suggesting that you only raise your hand to volunteer for a task or to ask a question. If you are trying to improve your speed and you want to be a Runner, the place to start is *not* by pooh-poohing ideas or even throwing out ideas of your own in a meeting, because you have not established a track record of actually doing the work in the past. If all you are doing is giving ideas, the team will perceive it as you coming up with more work for them to do. In order to start running, the place to do it isn't in the idea department; it's in the hard work department.

For example, we once decided to transform our school overnight into a carnival, which involved hanging five hundred yards of yellow, blue, and red drapes; transforming our classrooms into various scenes from the carnival; laying almost a ton of hay on the floor; and putting funhouse-themed decorations everywhere. For our lessons, we taught things that were necessary to run a carnival, but we included our content. For math class, students had to determine the square footage needed to house a carnival, and they had to create a working budget that included everything from the price of admission to all overhead costs. In art class, they had to build a clown costume; in history class, they learned the history of carnivals around the world; and in Language Arts, they created all of the advertisements. When it came time to transform the school overnight, it was a ton of work, and at midnight, I looked around and saw six staff members were still left, trying to make everything perfect. Let me tell you this: during the next meeting in which we are discussing taking on such a project, the ideas and comments of those six individuals carried the most weight. They proved they are "down for the down," and therefore they have earned a voice. Those who left at four that afternoon should hush.

And if you aren't going to be the one doing the work to fix any problem you choose to bring up in a meeting, you should hush too. If you aren't running or jogging, people may still appear to be listening to you in earnest, but they want you to hush too.

15

Stay in your lane

It was one of those days when the bus should have been roll-ing down the highway smoothly and steadily. Instead, Drew was annoyed to find he had to keep hitting the brakes to slow down for someone who was drifting around between lanes. Drew did not like the lane changers at all. To Drew's mind, they are members of a dangerous breed, made up of people who swerve constantly because they've lost focus. People think changing lanes will get you there faster, but Drew under-stands that is just an illusion. It's simple science, he thinks, that the shortest route from Point A to Point B is a straight line. It takes loyalty, patience, and faith to remain in your lane and stay focused on the road ahead of you—especially if

you happen to glance over and see a tempting stretch of open
road that you believe is calling your name. Drew fervently
hopes his team will not fall for that siren song. Focus is what
he needs from them. Sweet, sweet focus.

I know that we're all tempted to "change lanes" at times. Sometimes you'll be running along at a brisk clip, doing your job and doing it well, and you'll look over at the person in the next lane and see what she is—or isn't—doing. And then maybe your first instinct is to drift over into that lane and get involved, to somehow help that person do her job better, faster, or smarter.

Runners fall into this trap more often than you might think, because they are so focused on moving that bus along and always trying to pick up speed. But there's a fine line between helping the organization as a whole to accelerate and meddling in someone else's job. When you spend too much time focused on what others are doing, you risk losing sight of your own job, if only temporarily.

The shortest route from Point A to Point B is a straight line.

For example, when we first opened RCA we had a phenomenal employee who went above and beyond in her area as well as helping out in the classroom and with the afterschool programs. She really supported the students and was an awesome contributor. Every now and then, however, she would see something that she felt the need to check on, and I'd get an email from her that said something like "You might want to go ahead and arrange for security for that event next week" or "Who is going to do carpool on Thursdays now that so-and-so isn't doing it anymore?" Well, she didn't handle security issues or the carpool schedule—I did. And she was just about the best employee you could hope for, but I wanted to say to her, "Stay in your lane! I've got this."

Before RCA I worked with another teacher who is a giver. He loves to make sure that everybody's taken care of, and he loves to help people out. He's a Runner, but he'll look over at Joggers and Walkers who aren't going as fast and try to help them move faster. It's almost like he grabs hold of them and tries to pull them along—but it slows him down in the process. The others may speed up some, so he's clearly helping them. But now maybe he's jogging instead of running. It was frustrating for me because these kinds of efforts don't help the organization as a whole. I saw he wasn't really focused on completing his tasks because he was so busy helping others.

I see this happen in the business world as well. I had a friend who was trying to get a promotion. Every time we went out to dinner, she would talk about her colleagues, how she was helping them along, and how she'd pull the weight on certain projects. When someone in her department didn't know how to handle a situation with a client, she said, "Let's handle it this way" and stepped in and wrote an email for him. So when it came time for the promotion, she didn't get it—it went to one of the people she had helped so much. And I want to stress that it's good to support people, to mentor those with less experience. But you don't want to do it in ways that detract from your own performance.

Sometimes, when I see people switching lanes, I want to tell them, "You're too focused on all this stuff that's not your responsibility. If you put more focus on just making sure you handle all your own stuff, I think you'll be even more productive." I do expect my staff to support and uplift one another, but that should not happen to the detriment of your own list of goals and accomplishments. You want to cheer for everyone and assist when needed, but you don't want to do anyone's job for them, and you don't want to sacrifice your tasks to help others complete theirs. If everyone were to concentrate on accomplishing their own tasks and doing them well, they would go much faster than if they were drifting over to give their two cents about everybody else's tasks.

Don't drift into the next lane—keep your eyes on the road in front of you!

16

Change the conversation to change the culture

Holy negativity, Wanda is on a tirade again! She's ranting about the route, complaining about her colleagues, and whining about the weather they're driving in. If she rolls her eyes one more time, *thinks Joan,* they might just roll way far back into her head and stay there. *Even Ridley is tired of hearing it because, frankly, it's disrupting his nap.* When Wanda grumbles once again about the fog and drizzle they're passing through, Rufus decides he has to do something, anything, to put the brakes on the pessimism.

Sooo . . . here goes nothing . . . " 'THE SUN WILL COME OUT TOMORROW!' " Rufus belts out in a booming bari-tone that isn't quite right for the song. " 'Bet your bottom dollar that tomorrow there'll be suuuun!' "

If you are participating in negative conversations, stop. If someone brings up a sour topic, change the conversation or quickly bring up points like, "How can we make things bet-ter?" and "How can we make a positive change?"

I think it must be human nature that when someone tells us something horrible that happened to them that day, we then want to one-up them by telling something horrible that happened to us. For example, when Kim Bearden, the co-founder of our school, told me that she had to teach seven straight hours without even a bathroom break, I naturally told her that I taught even longer that day without a bath-room break *or* lunch. I think it's just natural for us to want people to know that our plight is worse than theirs.

In my mind, though, I visualize those conversations like digging a pothole. One person starts with a shovelful of neg-ativity, but the next person one-ups them and takes an even bigger chunk out of the hole. The process continues until you have a huge crater that you both are sitting in, depressed, low, and defeated. When someone tells you how hard their day was, quickly say, "I am so sorry to hear that, but can I tell you one great bright spot I had in my day?" Proceed to tell something good. And be forewarned that your colleague will want to pull you back in the hole and direct the conversation back to their horrible experiences. It's as if they are trying to win an award for "The Most Put-Upon Person on Earth." You have to make a decision to walk away from that poison or stay there and be pothole bait. Trust me, people will allow you to be a sponge, soaking up all their negativity. But remember, a full sponge doesn't move very quickly, and it will keep you from being able to run, or even walk.

Don't be someone's sponge.

My best friend, Amanda Nixon, is an entrepreneur in the area of specialty retail boutiques. Her vision includes a specific type of store environment and a culture of impeccable customer service, so she is always coaching her staff about how their conversation affects the customer's experience. Sometimes she'll hear a store employee chatting with a customer and saying things like "It's such beautiful weather today that I wish I could be outside" or "I'm tired from being on my feet all day." If you've ever worked in the retail or hospitality industries, maybe you've made similar small talk with your client base. It might seem harmless, but comments like that convey to your customers that you really don't want to be there helping them select the perfect gift or find a flattering fit or order the right wine to complement a meal. Yet, just by changing the conversation, you can change the mood.

It works the same way when you're moving toward a goal. When you're 75 percent of the way there, you can either focus on how far you have yet to go and lament the circumstances that have held you back. Or you can get all fired up and motivated to reach the final destination no matter what it takes—three-quarters of the work is done, so take time to congratulate yourself and your team for that, then brainstorm ways to cross the finish line.

A positive conversation brings positive results. It can empower everyone around you.

17

Allow the Runners
to reap the rewards

"But it isn't fair," *complains Wanda.* "I've worked here the longest, and therefore I've put in more miles than those kids have!" *Drew doesn't even try to explain, one more time, that it's not the miles logged but rather the miles-per-hour pace that counts. He is simply not one to reward longevity over performance. When he has a perk to hand out, he hands it to Rufus, who slows down long enough to express his appreciation for it and then takes off running again. Joan has already figured this out and has stepped up her game so*

she can earn her share of rewards as well—a strategy that
works better than complaining.

The Runner deserves the promotion. The Runner deserves the biggest office. If there is money for members of the team to get new computers, then the Runners deserve to have it. It always amazes me how team members in organizations will complain when they aren't selected for perks or opportunities. They view everyone in the organization as equal and so, therefore, they all should have just as much access to rewards. But that isn't so. You all aren't equal; some are working much harder and contributing much more, and those are the individuals who deserve more.

When I was teaching in North Carolina, the principal announced that she was going to send three representatives from the school to an educators' weekend retreat at NCCAT (North Carolina Center for the Advancement of Teaching). Okay, I sat bolt upright in my seat! I had been dying to go. As I looked around the room, I saw all kinds of teachers raising their hands that they wanted to attend, and in all honesty, I didn't know some of them could move that fast. I sat there thinking, *They sit on their tails all day; they don't deserve this experience*. But, astonishingly, Mrs. Roberson said she would put all the names in a hat and draw three. So essentially, this educators' retreat became a lottery instead of a reward for high achievers and top performers. Would I ever hand out perks this way? Not on your life, and I don't recommend that corporate leaders do so either.

If you know you're not a Runner and the boss has a perk that is coveted by all, you should back down. Don't even put yourself in the running for it. Remember, you *want* everyone in your organization to do well. If you're in the NBA, you want the most valuable player on your team. It's to your advantage to have the NBA's assist leader playing on your side. That's going to help you. My grandma always said that if you lift up the people around you, you lift up yourself as well. So you want to strive for a mentality and attitude where you're looking to uplift those in your organization—which I'm sure is not the case for 99 percent of people, because they're thinking if they support a Runner, it's like helping them to go farther, to get the promotion or the recognition. It doesn't have to be like that.

So please try to be happy for and supportive of the Runners who carry the lion's share of the work. Understand that they deserve the perk—and that you shouldn't even put yourself in the running for it. And don't forget that you can earn a perk for yourself by stepping up your game. Even before you're actually running, your boss may see your efforts and improvements and decide to reward you.

18

Exude a sense of urgency

Wanda is feeling unsettled lately. Drew has really brought about some changes since he came on as driver and Wanda is seeing the effects of that change. For one thing, she no longer automatically receives a raise based on her many years on the bus—most rewards now go to Rufus. Joan is also steadily picking up her pace; she seems to be coming into her own in this new environment. Wanda is still dragging her feet, yet she realizes with surprise that she really does want Drew's approval and would like to be rewarded for a job well done. But where to start? And then it just happened—BOOM! Drew made a simple request of her and, without thinking,

Wanda jumped to her feet and rushed off to complete the task, lickety-split. So THIS is what motivation feels like . . .

A quote my grandmother frequently used, and one of her favorite sayings was "People who walk slow ain't got nowhere to go."

If you are moving around your job in a stroll, it's going to appear to people that you are in no hurry to get anything done. If you're injured or if you have a physical limitation, that's one thing, but if you are able-bodied and still moving slowly, then the limitation will appear to be laziness. When you call on a Runner to help you out, he will walk with intensity and get there in a flash. A Jogger will move at a normal speed, and a Walker will hesitate, almost as if he is insulted that he is being summoned, and then he will move at a pace that is near death. Even though the actual amount of difference in time that the Runner gets there as opposed to the Walker may only be a couple of seconds, those seconds speak volumes and show respect, a strong work ethic, and a desire to contribute to the team.

Imagine that you're at a restaurant. You're seriously hungry. The waiter comes over, takes your order, and walks away, and then you notice that prior to submitting your food order, he goes to other tables to ask if they need anything and to remove their dishes. What in the world? Honestly, you are going to get your food at about the same time regardless, but that slight shift in the waiter's priorities can be annoying to no end.

Quite recently, I attended an event during which a nonprofit organization in Atlanta was unveiling its new head. I was in the auditorium when this person was introduced, and as she walked to the podium, she moved so slowly that I had a feeling I wasn't going to like her. It seemed obvious that she was enjoying the applause of the crowd, and she gradually took her time and almost strolled to the podium. I was thinking, *Uh-oh, this is not going to be good.* Because if you move that slowly in response to a vibrant introduction and a round of applause, then you will most certainly move slowly in everything you do. I have a feeling she won't last long in this position—and my intuition is based completely on the way she walked.

Keep that in mind when you are asked to complete a task, because your supervisor will know if you went directly to knock it out or if you made pit stops along the way. An employee at RCA, Kennedy Reddick, is a beast. He is in charge of the after-school programs, but he is also my assistant. When given a task, he does things so quickly it can be shocking. I was meeting with him and going over a list of tasks, and the second item on the list was renting a U-Haul truck. At the end of the meeting, I asked him to go ahead

and order the U-Haul first, and he said, "I already did." He
had pulled up the website and reserved it on his phone during the meeting right then and there, and I hadn't even realized it!

The third item on that list was to make an appointment
for me to get an X-ray on my elbow, which I'd injured in
a basketball game with the students. When the receptionist told him over the phone that they were booked solid for
the next two weeks, he got in his car, drove straight there,
and went to see her in person. He always wears the most
incredible suits, and he walks up to people, smiles the biggest smile, and says, "I'm not sure if you can help me or not,
but . . ." and just by saying it that way, people almost want
to prove that they can help him if they want to, and they
do! No surprise, the receptionist made the appointment for
the next day. This man knocks things out, but the best part
about it is that when he's given a task, nothing stands in his
way. He doesn't stop in the hall to talk with colleagues, he
doesn't complain or make excuses that a task is impossible;
he just finds a way and makes it happen, and he moves to do
it quickly.

I meet with my staff members individually every Thursday, and when we meet, we develop a list of tasks that we
need to complete. On the following Thursday, we go over
the previous list before compiling a new one. When every-

one I meet with has completed all of the tasks on the list, our bus is zooming! When half of the lists are completed, we are jogging. And when the list is spotty, we're walking or riding, and it leaves me with great concerns. But I can always rest assured that when I meet with Kennedy, his list is done without error, and most times he somehow manages to get it done early so that he can take on additional tasks. It's wonderful! There is no procrastination, there are no excuses, and nothing takes priority over his list. If you tackle your tasks in that manner, you're running! Don't delay the assignment, and the quicker you complete it, the more praise you will earn in the eyes of others.

> *A Rider thinks the list is not reasonable and will make excuses why the tasks couldn't be done.*
> *A Walker will finish a part of the list so that they don't get in trouble.*
> *A Jogger feels very content when the list is complete.*
> *A Runner wants to get the list finished quickly so that more can be done.*

19

Find solutions

The bus comes to a screeching halt. Okay, this has never happened before, but there is an entire flock of sheep in the road, in front of the bus. It's like a wall of wool, a bleating roadblock that the bus cannot get past. Everyone scrambles out, scratching their heads. Rufus stands on top of the bus to get a sense of how far and wide this problem extends. Joan grabs her iPad and starts googling for any kind of information that could shed some light on this very strange dilemma. Wanda looks to Drew, the driver, for direction. Ridley sits down on the curb and inspects his fingernails. "If we can get around this blockade within the next twenty minutes, I'll buy lunch for the rest of the week," says Drew.

When my students start to complain, I always tell them, "No excuses, only solutions." When staff members take on that attitude, it can really get the bus rolling faster.

If I meet with a team member and ask her to contact someone, it can be frustrating when I check back a week later and she tells me, "I emailed, but that person never wrote back." People seem to have forgotten the art of picking up a phone and calling someone. The fact is, if your first approach doesn't work, then you need to try another method.

We were in a staff meeting discussing the new class of students who would be entering our school. We were going to send them invitations to come to RCA for our annual meet-and-greet, where we introduce the new class to the entire school, but I had a better idea. I said:

"Hey, I have a plan. Why don't we find some dragon DNA, grow an adult dragon, have her lay eggs, and then crack the eggs open and fill them with candy and T-shirts that say, 'Class of 2018.' The dragon eggs will be perfect since our basketball team is the Blue Dragons! We can then bury the eggs in dirt inside big *Jurassic Park*–type crates and mail them to our new students in lieu of sending a normal invitation."

Well, my staff knows by now that I like to paint a picture and that I was basically telling them to dream big. Our task, then, was to figure out how to make the experience become a reality, and we had a budget of only seven dollars per student to do it. We spent about five to ten minutes discussing ideas, and it became apparent it was just going to be impossible. But right when we were about to abandon the idea, Hope King, one of the incredible Runners on our staff, said, "I'll do it." I asked, "How?" and she replied, "I'll get the DNA, I'll hatch the eggs, I'll get them to the students. I'll find a way." Now, I could not envision a possible way for it to happen, but she said she had it, so I let her take on the project, and we moved on.

One week later, I walked into the library to see thirty incredibly well crafted *Jurassic Park*–style crates. Hope had gotten the wood donated from Home Depot and had assembled a team of individuals who built the crates by hand. She had purchased cheap bags of artificial grass to fill the crates. She ordered massive Easter eggs online, but when they arrived, she knew the bright pink color just wouldn't work, so she spray painted them greenish-brown. She filled them with candy and "Class of 2018" T-shirts that she arranged to have donated by our T-shirt partner, Shirt Shanty. When she didn't like that the crates looked brand-new, she painted and distressed them so that they looked worn and aged. It was brilliant, and it was all done within the budget of seven dollars a crate. Hope then stood before me and hung her head as she said, "It is going to cost us $20 a crate to mail these suckers." I said, "That's okay, instead of mailing them we could just hand them out to the students when they arrive at RCA." But she refused that idea and added, "I'm going to hand deliver each crate to each child's front doorstep in the middle of the night."

What a runner. In typical Hope King fashion, she found a way.

When you become known for offering up solutions and finding ways to get something done, you raise your worth in the organization and become the most valuable player in your supervisor's eyes. The more limits that are placed on you, like a tight budget or quick deadline, the harder you'll work to find a solution. When others can't find a way, but you can, trust me, your initiative will always be recognized and rewarded.

no achievements. *She's never been the most valuable player or a top performer. It may be time for her to check her entitlement at the door.*

Why do we even have to have this conversation about a bus? What has happened to America, and why isn't everyone inspired to run naturally? We are a nation built by people with a tremendous work ethic, people who weren't afraid of a challenge. Now, it seems Runners are becoming the rarity, and everyone feels they are owed something. And the sense of entitlement that is so commonplace in America starts with you. No one promised you that you will have the job you have forever.

During the first year of RCA's existence, we decided to give the staff bonuses in December. The team was overjoyed, and many cried. Their outpouring of appreciation was heartwarming, and we knew we had made the right decision to give the bonuses. The next year, the reaction was similar but not quite as profound. In each subsequent year, the reaction grew less and less appreciative, because the bonus became expected. I occasionally even heard people talk about what they were going to do with their bonus, and I had to point out that the bonus wasn't guaranteed; it was something we did when we could.

That particular year, we realized we weren't going to be able to give out the bonus because the economy was strug-

20

Realize you are not entitled to this job

Wanda has a résumé that shows she is smart. She went to an Ivy League university, received a scholarship to study abroad, and earned an internship at one of the world's most innovative corporations. She's well read and well traveled, she plays the cello, she can hold a conversation in French. And she's pretty sure anyone would look at her résumé and hire her in a heartbeat, based on the names of the places she has worked and studied. So Wanda is shocked to find that's not the case. It turns out that while she has credentials, she has

gling and we simply didn't have the money. In the end, however, we sat down with our board members and came up with a way to make it happen. It didn't come without sacrifices, and the bonuses weren't as large as they had been in the past. The Runners, however, in typical Runner fashion, showed the same amount of appreciation and thanks that they had shown in the past. The other members of the team sent emails like, "Thanks for the bonus," and then a few didn't even mention it. The bonus had become something they expected, and that is how many people view their jobs. They think they deserve the job and that they are entitled to it, and once that mind-set is there, the work ethic of those individuals tends to decline.

What has led us to this entitled state of being? I think the answer lies in the way we are raising and educating our children in America.

There is a wave of thought that we must do all we can to keep the self-esteem of children intact—to the point that we aren't being realistic with kids about their abilities. Why does every child on the Little League team now receive a trophy? They all ain't that good. You know who should get the trophy? The most valuable player. And when your child cries, "Why didn't I get a trophy?" you should respond, "Because you aren't the MVP." Period. End of discussion. We are simply giving children too much, and when kids receive things without having to work for them, they begin to expect things for nothing. They feel entitled and believe things are owed to them, and they eventually end up living at home with their parents at the age of twenty-six, sitting on the couch all day, and wondering, *Why doesn't the world love me?*

History teaches us that when a civilization rises to supremacy that it will eventually decline when the youth, the brain trust, don't have to work as hard. When they aren't challenged, they relax because they are given more than they need. They grow to feel entitled and lack a work ethic. That is the situation in America now. We're already twenty-seventh in the world in terms of our education system. Where will we be years from now as long as we continue to raise a soft, wussified generation of children? We are giving them too much and teaching them that it is their right to receive things without working for them.

This sense of entitlement has transferred to the business world. I hear stories now about the youngest college graduates going into job interviews and saying things like "I'll probably have your job in two years." Yes, they have that much confidence. Then they get hired, and that confidence doesn't translate to performance. It's a crisis. They don't like to be criticized. They don't want anyone pointing out that they aren't perfect. They make excuses: *In my defense . . . no one told me . . . I didn't see that in the handbook . . .* They will make a small contribution to a project and expect to receive a large amount of praise. The reason for this is that they haven't been made to work very hard in our education system, yet they have received numerous awards for their work.

If you grew up receiving a trophy just for playing on the team, let me give you a reality check: That will not happen in the workplace. This is capitalism, not socialism. You have to do more than just show up to be rewarded. Please, be grateful for your job. Be thankful to be a part of a team. Work to earn actual recognition and praise, because nothing is promised to you.

When a society coddles the brain trust, it marks the beginning of its decline.

21

Be credible

Today is a big day, and Drew needs the support of his whole team. Ridley has vowed over and over again he will be there at 8:00 a.m. sharp, yet Drew feels uneasy. How likely is it that this will actually happen? Should he have told Ridley to be there at 7:30, to allow a little wiggle room when he's late? It's funny, thinks Drew, how some people can make the most basic promises, and no one really believes them. Ridley says he'll stay awake all day, and it sounds like a tall tale. Yet Rufus can talk your ear off about how he's going to break the sound barrier someday and you sit up and listen and believe in him . . . because Rufus is a guy who delivers.

As with any visionary, some of the things I say I am going to do sound far-fetched, and I have to work really hard to ensure that I back up my statements. For four years, I told my staff I was going to put a huge dragon skeleton in our school someday. I don't know how seriously anyone took me, because dragons are supposed to be fictional and all, but guess what? We now have a two-story dragon skeleton towering over our new cafeteria in the brand-new addition at RCA. It was a long-standing vision I had, to add this magical touch to our facility, and I had to wait for the right time to make it happen, but it finally did happen. During our sneak peek event, when we unveiled the new addition to our students, parents, and staff, people kept coming up to me and saying "You really did it!" and "This is so inspiring." People were inspired, because they love when someone makes good on what they said they were going to do. The facility also has, as promised, a two-story slide, fire painted on the gym floor, magical portals, a bungee jump in the library, secret passageways, and a Harry Potter great hall—all promises that were fulfilled. Now, I hope I was credible to my staff long before these items came to life, but I recognize the importance of reinforcing my credibility as often and any way that I can.

Credibility might be the single most desirable trait you can cultivate in yourself, because it encompasses so much. When you are credible, people know they can rely on you as a team member—and as a leader, when you're called upon to lead.

We have a rule at RCA that if you tell a child you're going to do something, then you have to do it, because kids are let down far too often already. So if we tell the students we're going to take them somewhere, we take them there without fail. We're also very careful about how and when we use the word *promise* with the children, because sometimes things happen that interfere with plans and promises, and we don't want to break a firm promise.

In many people's minds, a promise is an oath, and if you tell your boss "I promise I'm going to have the report ready and on your desk at nine a.m.," then you want to do all you can to stick to what you say. Once you've lost credibility by failing to deliver, it can be very difficult to get it back. The number one rule of being credible is this: *honor your commitments and don't make commitments you can't keep.*

We hire a company called ImageMaster to produce all our videos and promotional pieces. They are phenomenal at what they do, but one of the main reasons we love them so much is that they always hit their deadlines. If they say it will be ready on Friday, it's ready on Friday. I never have to worry about it or be concerned that they're not going to deliver. There have been times when we bid the projects to other companies, and some of them promised to have our projects completed quicker than ImageMaster. Their quotes always come in cheaper, and it seemed like a better idea to go with them. It never failed, however, that the product wasn't delivered on time and the quality just wasn't there. So even though ImageMaster may take longer, we trust that when they say it will be ready, that it will be ready. Leaders are willing to pay more for credibility and quality, and when you have the two combined, you're setting yourself up for a lot of success.

Credibility has a lot to do with being reliable, but it's even more than that. You can demonstrate credibility by taking responsibility for your mistakes and finding ways to correct any errors you make. By making sure that any information you provide is factual and up to date. By being the person who knows where to find answers. By setting wise priorities so you're not spinning your wheels on tasks that don't provide value to the organization. If you value your own reputation for being credible, you will communicate that to your teammates and your boss through all your actions and words. People will know instinctively they can trust you to come through for them.

I think what makes an effective leader—whether it's a CEO or a twenty-five-year old leading a first project—is that people on the team have to believe that the individual in charge is leading for the right reason and with the right intent in their heart. People want to be led by others who they believe have their best interests in mind and the best interests of the organization and not as a method of self-promotion. We want strong, passionate, confident leaders, but ones who also understand that the organization is bigger than one individual—and that includes the founders of the firm. When people are being managed by others who they trust and believe in, they are then ready to be led and will buy in to the project, mission, goal, and objective; and the leader will be successful because his teammates will not allow him to be anything else.

22

Pay attention to details

Rufus hasn't always cruised along as smoothly as a Tour de France cyclist at the pinnacle of his career. It's hard to believe, but he used to hit bumps in the road so hard that he'd feel his teeth rattling in his head. Gradually, Rufus figured out lots of little ways to improve the ride, just by paying attention to what people responded to, what worked and what didn't. He had to learn how to pace himself during a steep climb. When to shift gears to keep the engine at the perfect equilibrium. Where the worst potholes were located, so he could plan to avoid them without having to swerve or slow down at the last minute. All of these things made a difference. They really did.

The Runners at RCA are always looking for ways to step things up, to rev the engine, to improve the quality of the ride. They're always asking themselves *What can we do to make this a little bit better?* It's about an attention to detail, but not in a nitpicky way. Instead, it's more about finding ways to uplift people by fine-tuning all the little details to make every experience warmer and more inviting.

Ms. Renita Mosley is our office manager. She sits at the front desk and greets everyone who visits RCA. One day I said to her, "I have an idea. What if every time someone walks in the door, you get up and walk around the desk to greet them personally? And what if you give them a hug, especially if it's someone new and we don't know them?" She said, "You mean every person?" I said, "Yes. Anyone new or anyone who's come in before, you should get up from your desk." A lot of people come to visit our school, and it's a lot of effort, but she said, "Let's do it." And I believe that personalized greeting has made a visit to RCA an exceptional experience. It's the same thing when Ms. Mosley answers the telephone. She used to say "Ron Clark Academy." Now she says, "Good morning. You've reached the Ron Clark Academy, and this is Renita."

It's those small, subtle touches that make everything better. If you work in a service industry, you can always find ways to enhance the customer experience—think of it as that Godiva chocolate on the hotel pillow every night. I recently went for a haircut, and as soon as I sat down someone asked if he could bring me a Coke or a cup of coffee. I thought that was really cool—it was a step up.

You can also make a product seem more appealing by adjusting the little details. It's all in the presentation. We sell T-shirts in our school store and they used to just be folded flat, the way your mom would fold your clean laundry at home. Then Chrissi Major, our marketing coordinator, had an idea to roll up the T-shirts and secure them with a little band of decorated paper that has "Ron Clark Academy" printed on it. And all of a sudden we went from selling five T-shirts every Friday, when the visiting educators come through, to selling fifty. Fifty T-shirts! It blew us away, because we realized the product hadn't changed at all—it was all about the way we presented it. My Runners are always looking for ways to make things like that happen.

A while back, we knew that one of our business clients was going to be in Atlanta. This is a very important corporate sponsor for us. We knew which hotel he was staying at, and we knew that he loved the show *Wicked* and that he considers 17 to be his lucky number. So we had chocolates made in the shape of the *Wicked* characters and the number 17, and we created a gift basket with these custom chocolates and an RCA T-shirt. We delivered it to his hotel, so it was there sitting on the counter when he checked in that night. He told us he was blown away by this gesture. He went on and on about how he travels around the country and deals with major corporations but that no one had ever presented him with such a thoughtful gift. And within one month his company made a donation to our school in the amount of a half million dollars. Now, I'm not saying the basket was all that led to the donation, but it was definitely part of the appeal, part of the effort, part of who we strive to be at RCA. It's about attention to detail, appreciation, and excellence, and it pays off.

Overall in any organization, Runners and Joggers tend to be more concerned with the details. They realize that small things can be important, can demonstrate respect or a work ethic, just as much as larger things do. I think a lot of Riders and Walkers have a misconception that they cannot move up in the organization unless they make a huge sale or woo a big client. They think they have to do something enormous and that seems overwhelming so instead they do nothing. Don't make that mistake. Turn your eye to the little details and find ways to step everything up a notch.

Potholes and roadblocks

Avoid these common mistakes that can keep you from being a Runner.

1. Don't see and spread the negative.

I work at one of the most electric and uplifting places in the world, yet we have problems. Every school, every business, every organization has problems, and we all have the opportunity to choose how we realize that truth. I have worked with some who think that in order to improve the organization it's their duty to point out everything they see that is wrong. They share with everyone and are always noting the negative. That is toxic and will do nothing but slow everyone down and lower productivity. Runners tend to look around at the organization and notice all the blessings, success, and beauty around them. They want to add to that productive spirit, and they will find ways to do so.

The best news is that you have a choice. What do you choose to see?

2. Don't make excuses.

Some who don't run will try to find reasons to excuse themselves from going faster. They will often say they are trying to have a work-life balance or that their children and other family members take precedent over work. Honestly, they're right, and I wouldn't encourage anyone to put work over their family, but there is a way to do both. I have worked with teachers who have large families and that keeps them from doing activities after school and on weekends to support our organization; however, when they are at work from 8 a.m. to 5 p.m. they are positive, productive, and hardworking. These teachers may not be able to take kids on trips on Saturday afternoons, but if they teach with their hearts and look their students directly in the eyes, they will be making a bond that is equally profound. If your family obligations keep you from doing all you want, just make sure that when you are at work that you are there. Be present! Be on point when it counts!

3. Don't let the drama on your personal bus affect your work bus.

We all have a work bus and a personal bus, and many of you have made some bad choices that have left you with a personal bus that isn't going where you want it to go. You are in a relationship that isn't working for you. You are tired, hurt, and in pain, and because of that you can't be all you should be at work. I have been there, and it's miserable. I encourage you, as you sit on your personal bus, to turn around and look at the person in your relationship. OMG, it's a Rider. You have chosen to be in a relationship with a Rider. You keep telling yourself that if you run hard enough that you can make it work. You are convinced that eventually that Rider is going to run with you. Well, I have news for you. Riders can never run. Riders can't even jog. The most you will get is that maybe a Rider can walk, but Riders can never do more than that. This is why your relationship isn't going where you want it to go. You need to step off that bus and get on another one with someone who will go at your speed. Stop lying to yourself and telling yourself it's going to get better; it's not. And you are wasting time and expending so much energy to try to get your personal bus to run that you don't have the energy to give to your work bus. Don't let that happen to you! Be very, very careful who you allow on your personal bus.

4. Don't assume you're awesome.

Often, people will assume they are doing an awesome job and that their boss is content with their performance. When their boss doesn't recognize them, they become disgruntled and feel they aren't getting the attention and praise they deserve. In actuality, the reason they aren't getting praise for being awesome is because . . . they aren't awesome. If you feel you aren't being recognized, a likely reason is that the job you're doing isn't as great as you think it is or that, while you may be doing some things well, other aspects of your performance are lacking.

5. Don't just be good, be efficient!

In the end, it comes down to productivity. How much are you accomplishing? You may be doing a good job, but are you also making sure that you are getting the job done? For example, if you were riding a bus to work and the bus driver was really nice with a great personality, you'd enjoy the ride more. But if that same driver took a long time to close the door, to map the route, to collect the money, and to get to her next stop, you'd probably be upset, especially if it makes you fifteen minutes late to work. When I check in at airline counters, I can feel how stressed people are. They are in a hurry to get through security and get to their flights; and I see how some counter workers have an attitude that says, "I am not going to be made to rush. You aren't going to stress me out." They move slowly and in a methodical fashion, and it adds to the problem. Some, however, are moving quickly, knocking things out, and multitasking to get the job done. If you want to run, you need to handle everything you do with a smile, a positive spirit, and an energy that leads to efficiency.

PART III

How to Map the Route

My friend David Krantz is the CEO of a company known as YP. You probably knew it as the Yellow Pages, and maybe you used it to look up a phone number when you wanted to have a pizza delivered. But then the world changed, and the big yellow book lost ground to online search engines and mobile apps—so the company had to change, too, in order to stay relevant. David completely rebranded and transformed the culture of the company. It has a whole new vibe, starting with the name YP to take the focus away from pages that are printed on paper. Today, YP.com and YPmobile are leading players in the field of local advertising and local search results. It's a fun, modern, digital organization to work for, and it's all because David had a clear vision and top-notch skills as a Driver. He had what it takes to bring about change.

You don't have to be the CEO of a Fortune 500 company or the principal of a school to be a leader and drive a transformation. Sometimes you're not the official Driver, but you're called upon to drive anyway—like Sandra Bullock in the action-thriller movie *Speed*. When her character, Annie, found out a bomb would detonate and kill everyone on a city bus (yes, this movie has an actual bus!) if she let the speed fall below 50 mph, she rose to the occasion and drove that bus, navigating through traffic jams on the LA freeways and zooming around city streets without running anyone over, all while maintaining the right speed.

You can rise to the occasion, too. Leadership is a skill that you can develop in yourself, over time. If you have passion about something and a way with people, you can lead. You can head up a committee or take on a special project—not only at work, but at your school, church, or neighborhood association as well. You can take on the role of Driver for any number of groups or projects and can steer that particular bus effectively by modeling the behaviors you want your team members to have.

Without a doubt, being the Driver at RCA is a tremendous amount of work. It's all worth it to me, however, because I'm trying to build something real and lasting, something that will have an impact on the way we educate children long after I'm gone. Along the way, I've gotten a lot better at driving this bus and steering my team toward excellence, and in this section I'm going to share some strategies with you so you can become a more effective Driver as well.

Are you ready to take the wheel? Here we go!

23

Allow Runners to shine

The district manager came along last week to observe Drew's team and make recommendations. "That guy Rufus is up-staging you," he told Drew in confidence. "If I were you, I'd be worried he'll go after your job—and I'd be trying to find ways to slow him down a little." But Drew isn't buying it, not in the least. Drew's job is to keep the bus moving, as quickly and efficiently as possible. To slow Rufus down would mean the entire organization would lose ground. Nope, it's better for everyone that he continue to let Rufus run like the wind, even allow him to test out his inventive new methods to gain speed. Drew knows that his own special talent is managing talent. So shine on, Rufus. Shine on!

I was young, twenty-three years old, and filled with wild ambition. It was my first teaching experience, and boy, was I wide open, dressing in costumes, using music and chants, and even teaching a geography lesson while completely upside down in order to get my students to focus. My principal called me in the office, looked me dead in my eyes, and said, "Ron, I *love* it! The kids adore you. You've got no discipline problems. The parents are thrilled. And your test score results are outstanding. Please continue to do what you are doing . . . but can you close your door?"

My eyes were as wide as saucers as I responded, "Huh, am I being too loud?" And she responded, "No, but you are causing some problems." She said the other teachers were complaining because their students were saying they wished they were in my class. She said parents were calling her and asking to have their children transferred to my classroom. Her last words to me were, "Definitely keep doing what you're doing, but if you can keep the door closed, it will be better for everyone."

I said, "Oh, yes, ma'am. I am so sorry, and I'll close my door." I walked out of the office with a mixture of anger and sadness welling up inside of me. *Why do the ones who do the most have to downplay? Shouldn't the others have to step up their game instead of me hiding mine?*

It is very important, for the good of your organization, that you let your Runners shine. Don't hide their light under a bushel basket! If you ask your Runners to hide their success or to do their important work under cover, you make them feel unappreciated and that can cause them to decelerate—or even to hop aboard another bus that is moving at the speed of light.

At previous jobs where I was surrounded by Riders and Walkers, I felt defeated and lost. It was as if all the tires on the bus were flat. I realized there was no way in hell I could move that bus. As a business leader, do you really want your top performers to feel this way? If you're losing key talent to your competitors, this may be part of the problem.

I've been to schools where there really aren't any Runners, but there are a lot of Joggers who consider themselves to be top performers. If a true Runner comes onboard in an environment like that, she will very likely be perceived as a threat. The Joggers may band together to discount the hard work of that Runner. When you only have one Runner in your organization, you have to work hard to protect that individual because she is in a very vulnerable position. I have visited more than three hundred schools in the country, in all fifty states, and I almost always have someone come up to me and say, "I'm struggling and I want to quit because I'm the only one here trying to go above and beyond the basic requirements of the job."

So how can you let your Runners shine, without stirring the pot and creating resentment among your other workers?

This is a complicated question without a single good answer, because there are so many variables. But the last thing you want to do is to tell your top performer to close his door. This is like asking an Olympic-bound track athlete to slow down a little, so the others on the team won't feel bad about themselves. It's like suggesting to Einstein that he keep those ideas to himself for now, because the world isn't ready for them. It's just plain crazy how many leaders try to reduce the visibility of a top performer.

Don't hide a Runner's light under a bushel basket!

My friend Amanda, an entrepreneur and boutique owner, has told me how she lets her Runners shine. At her stores she prefers to put the strongest salespeople at the front of the store, where they can warmly greet every customer who enters and use their exceptional customer service skills to meet a client's needs. This practice not only boosts sales but also enhances the boutique's reputation for personalized service, friendliness, and attention to detail. Yet Amanda has seen other retail managers shoot themselves in the foot by trying to slow down a Runner with instructions like "Let someone else help the next customer." To give all of the sales associates an opportunity, they will rotate customers, but that, in turn, slows down sales and productivity; it's all in an effort to be fair to those who aren't talented. It makes no sense. She's also seen store managers put the brakes on a staff member who wanted to go the extra mile for a client by staying thirty minutes later or offering more specialized service. Holding back a top performer like this does nothing to further the goals of the organization as a whole.

As a leader, every now and then you might end up with a staff member you feel is more energetic or talented than you are. Please don't make the mistake of viewing your star Runner as a threat to you. Get over it and figure out the best way to leverage that talent for the good of the organization. Don't be tempted to take credit for your top Runner's best ideas and achievements. Give her the visibility she deserves and help those who are jealous or who seek to marginalize her contributions to get over it as well.

My best friend from childhood, Matt Crisp, built a multimillion-dollar company called eVestment from the ground up. I am so proud of his success, but I am more impressed by how he leads his organization. He is focused on encouraging the members of his team to shine; he wants them to feel empowered and confident. One of the main ways he recognizes his Runners is simply by rewarding them throughout the year with additional responsibility and giving them the opportunity to work on influential projects within the firm—projects they would ordinarily not have the opportunity to work on at that particular stage of their career. This has proven particularly effective with his under-thirty associates.

In addition, he has an anniversary celebration every June to celebrate the business and also to recognize seven individuals in different categories who represent their core values, which are: excellence, focus, integrity, innovation, teamwork, and attitude/humility. Nominations for each category are done by the associates in the organization (*not* by the founders). There are generally five finalists selected in each category, and then the voting happens—again, at the associate level (*not* by the founders). During the anniversary celebration, each of the founders takes two categories and speaks for three to five minutes about the winner of each award, brings them up, and presents them with an award in front of the entire organization.

Nice, right? But this company goes a step further. They also communicate statistics about the number of different associates who were nominated by their peers, which is generally in the 50- to 60-percent range of their total associate base. They have found (and truly believe) that communicating to people that just being nominated is an honor, being a finalist is a big honor, and to win the award voted on by your peers is the ultimate recognition that you were a Runner in that category during the past twelve months. These awards are all around the office and on display in people's work areas, so that everyone can always see the recognition of their efforts.

They also have a seventh award called the Founders Award, which goes to longer-term associates who have contributed significantly to the overall growth of the organization, have helped mentor the next level of leaders, and are well thought of by their peers. This is a truly special award, and people now view it as such and strive to be there long enough and contribute in a way that affords them the opportunity to be considered for this award. Finally, they offer stock option/equity participation in the firm for every associate at any level, and the stock options are granted free to associates at no investment of their own. Approximately 85 percent of current associates are stock option owners in the company, and they know that, as the company grows because of their efforts running every single day, that it will likely turn into a significant payout to them individually at some point in the not-so-distant future.

Another way they look to allow Runners to shine is by empowering them. Matt and his team are always looking for ways to encourage associates at all levels of the organization to make their own decisions based on well-thought-out logic and rationales. At their 2013 year-end company-wide, strategic meeting, they handed out customized poker chips to every associate as a symbol that they wanted them to take risks or make bets in areas they felt strongly about, without having to run it by their higher ups. The thought was that every associate at any level of the organization has the capacity to make good decisions—to be a Runner. So these poker chips were meant to be a physical reminder that it's okay to take a risk or make a decision and just own it, whether it turns out to be right or not. As long as the thought that went into the decision was sound (and the result of the decision was not going to bring down the entire company!), risk taking was encouraged. To use a sports analogy (because Matt loves sports), they want people "to play to win, rather than play *not* to lose."

24

Help Joggers to be their best selves

Joan has never been the fastest member of the team, but she does a great job overall. And Drew has noticed lately that Joan's big thing is safety procedures. She not only goes over every safety checklist at the beginning of every route, but she stays current on the latest research and is always quoting a new study about promising new safety technologies—like collision mitigation systems. Drew doesn't quite understand how anyone could be so infatuated with what he thinks of as "seatbelts and airbags," but he decides to let Joan follow her

*passion. He designates her as Safety Chief and gives her a
budget that she can use to optimize the bus's safety protocols.
It can't hurt, given Rufus's goal to break the sound barrier.
Plus, Joan has a new gleam in her eye these days . . .*

I appreciate my Joggers; I'm not going to lie. I appreciate
them because, for the most part, they do a great job and,
honestly, I let a lot go with Joggers because they are definitely
moving the bus in the right direction. Sure, I wish they were
Runners, but it's nearly impossible to have an organization
made up entirely of Runners—so I think business leaders are
better served by learning to work with their Joggers and fig-
uring out ways to boost their performance.

As the Driver, you have to treat your Joggers in a certain way. They need to be coddled a little bit more than the
Runners do; they need to be validated. So instead of focusing on things they aren't doing well, which is not going to
work, I tend to let them know what I like about their performance. In Part II, I talked a lot about how the majority
of the perks should go to the Runners, so I want to stress
that this doesn't mean you should always withhold rewards
from Joggers. If they've come from an environment where
they were rewarded and praised for doing one huge project
each year, they may think an occasional energy spurt is what
you expect as well, so you'll want to find ways to reward

them for and incentivize them to maintain a high level of energy that is consistent.

If you have several Runners on your team and only a couple of Joggers, it's very likely the Joggers will be inspired to run just by the company they are keeping, and that can make a huge difference. They will work harder to keep up, because Runners can generate enthusiasm and energy. If that's the case, a bit of targeted coaching on your part might be all a Jogger needs to start running.

You may also be able to get a Jogger fired up by aligning her duties with whatever she's best at or passionate about— in essence, giving the Jogger something she can run with. When you find a project that's a good fit, you tap into the Jogger's internal motivations. So if you manage a retail store, for example, you might find that a member of your staff is not a top seller but has a knack and a passion for visual merchandising. By giving her extra duties in that area, you give her more excitement and a sense of ownership over how she can personally help the organization move forward. She may not be running overall, but she's running when it comes to creating beautiful product displays or store windows.

While Runners have an instinctive confidence that they're moving in the right direction, Joggers are a bit more uncertain. They hope they're right, and they think they're right, and they're going for it, but they're still a little unsure.

And that's exactly why praise and appreciation go a long way with Joggers. If you can give them that extra affirmation that they're going in the right direction, they're going to go faster. The main thing slowing them down in the first place is that little bit of hesitation they are prone to. So be sure to check in with them more often than you do with your Runners and give them more guidance.

and show her a few simple little tricks . . . and the results are
fantabulous!

Sometimes I wonder how many Walkers grew up without a role model who could demonstrate a strong work ethic. For me, that role model was my mom. She worked all day, every day, at a $28K job, and then many nights a week I'd see her sitting at the kitchen table at home till eleven at night working on the company's payroll. She didn't get paid extra for this. She just wanted to make sure everything was perfect, that everyone's hours were totaled just right, and that all the withholdings were accurate. At one point, my mom had accrued 572 hours of overtime for which she could have requested a check. When I turned sixteen, she wanted to help me buy a car, a run-down, cheap 1979 yellow Ford Pinto so that I could have transportation to a job washing dishes at a local restaurant. She asked her company for $600 in overtime pay. They gave it to her, $600 for 572 hours of time. I said to her, "Mom, that is like a dollar per hour. Mom, that's horrible. Why would you take so little money?" She said, "Because it wasn't about the money. I wanted to do a good job and no one approved for me to work those hours; I just did it because it needed to be done." So I grew up witnessing that type of work ethic firsthand.

When you're the Driver in an organization and you have a Walker on your team, you need to be very clear about dem-

25

Show Walkers how to improve

Now that he has Rufus and Joan performing at ever-higher levels, Drew is turning his attention to Wanda. When he first came onboard, he had naturally just assumed that, as the slowest member of the team, Wanda was simply unmotivated. Now he's not so sure that there aren't other issues slowing her down. For one thing, she doesn't seem to know what kind of running shoes to wear, in order to light a fire in her step. And she has pacing issues, the kind of thing you could correct just by repeating a jump-rope rhyme to yourself until the rhythm becomes second nature to you. One day, he puts the bus on autopilot so he can run alongside Wanda

onstrating your values. You have to show them, *This is what I expect. This is how Runners perform*. And for some of them, it may be like they're seeing it for the first time.

I personally can remember what it's like to see positive, effective behaviors modeled for me in a way I could emulate. When I was seventeen years old, I started waiting tables at a pizza restaurant called The Legend. I thought I was a great waiter. I thought I was the best. Miss Brenda, the manager, actually told me I was the best waiter on her staff. Then I left and went to work for The River Forest Manor, and there was a server there named Cindy who was just phenomenal. She was engaging. She laughed and joked with the customers. She just had a way about her. I noticed that when Cindy took an order, she listened and looked the customer right in the eye, instead of looking down at a notepad. It was an emotional connection. I thought to myself, *I'm going to start doing that*. And once I did, my tips improved and I got better at connecting with the customers. And yet, I had started out thinking I was already great, but I just didn't know any better *because I had never seen anything better*. I had actually been a Walker without realizing it.

So you might have some Walkers in your organization, and you're really frustrated. You want them to jog, you want them to run. Why won't they? Sometimes it just comes down to this: *they just don't know what they don't know*. In some cases, if you can demonstrate a more effective way of doing things, a Walker is going to move faster for you. Of course, the success of this strategy depends on the willingness and ability of the Walker to learn, grow, and improve and it probably works best with younger workers who have ambition and potential but need some help to get up and running.

Now Riders are a different story. I honestly just want to tell you to fire all of them and move on to the next chapter, but I know that can sometimes be difficult to do, particularly in areas like education, where the tenure process protects ineffective teachers like an iron fortress. It may be possible to get a Rider to walk. But remember way back in chapter 5, where I told the story about the teacher who sat all day on the "stool of drool" and drove her students into a coma? I put a lot of effort into getting her up off that stool, only to see that my efforts and my minimal results had virtually no effect at all on the organization as a whole. When it comes to the Riders on your team, you'll have to decide for yourself if it's best to kick them off the bus or if you think they are capable of improving to the point they make a worthwhile contribution.

One of my favorite strategies for maximizing the contributions of Walkers and Riders is to delegate the grunt work to them. When everyone else is running at top speed and we have many miles yet to go in order to accomplish a goal, the Walkers and Riders are the most expendable members of the team. I'm not going to pull a Runner off course to have her pump the gas, for example, so I'm constantly directing the Walkers to those tasks. When they don't volunteer to do them, I'm quick to say, "Hey, could you help us out?," "Could you do that?," "Would you mind?," "If you could take care of that, that'd be awesome."

When it comes right down to it, you, as the Driver, are the best person to decide how to deal with the Walkers on your team. Some of them probably have potential, while others may not. You have to weigh the effort it will take to get them to pick up their feet and then decide if your time and energy would be best used elsewhere.

26

Equip people to meet your expectations

Drew's little experiment with Wanda has paid off handsomely. Just by running alongside her and showing her a few simple tricks of the trade, he's helped her boost her performance tremendously. Not only is she moving faster, but she also seems to have new pride in herself. Drew decides to do whatever he can, anything possible, to help everyone on the team be the best they can be. And he's starting with the most excellent equipment that money can buy. High-tech running shoes with self-adjusting laces. Wristbands that measure

heart rate and acceleration. Electronic gait analysis devices.
It's time to empower everyone!

There is a certain philosophy in education that I despise, and it's called "teaching to the middle." It's based on the notion that if you set the bar too high, the slowest students will be left in the dust—so to keep that from happening, teachers should lower the bar for every student. The problem with this is that our brightest, most talented students are bored instead of challenged. They never achieve their full potential, which becomes detrimental not only to our education system but to our society as a whole.

I firmly believe my students' success comes from my personal philosophy of teaching to the top and never lowering expectations. I want every student at RCA to be challenged, to be inspired to reach ever-higher levels. Now, clearly, if you're going to raise the bar for every child, then you have to figure out ways to lift them up to that level or many will fail. If you're going to teach eighth-grade algebra to fifth-graders, you have to help them rise to the challenge. And that's exactly what we do at RCA. We teach a rigorous curriculum. We lay out clear expectations. We never lower a goal. The key is we give our students a high level of support and the tools they need to succeed.

This principle applies to your business as well. It's not enough to set lofty goals for your team and leave them sitting there, scratching their heads over how they will double sales next month or improve customer satisfaction ratings over the next year. You have to equip your team to meet those expectations. And the first step in doing that is to communicate the expectation very specifically.

Let me give you an example. At RCA, we depend on a high level of support from the students' parents, and we cannot do what we do every day and every year without that support. So we set the bar high. At the beginning of each school year, we ask all of our parents to sign a contract. We tell them very clearly what we expect from them, that when they sign on the dotted line, they are committing to have their kids at school on time every day, to attend school functions on a regular basis, and to contribute forty hours of service to the school each year. No parent has ever fallen short. And do you know why that is? Because we let them know we expect it. I tell them exactly what I need, right down to the number of hours I need them to be at the school lending a helping hand, and they rise to the occasion.

After you set the bar and lay out clear expectations, you often have to fire up your team so they're excited about reaching the goal. I know you can find a way to do this because I really *did* figure out a way to teach eighth-grade algebra to my fifth-graders—by using music and dance to engage the students and make difficult concepts come alive. It wasn't easy, but one of our core values at RCA is to never lower a goal, so I worked hard to find methods and techniques that would be effective (and you can read about the whole process in my book, *The End of Molasses Classes: Getting Our Kids Unstuck*).

This is what a good Driver does—he uplifts people so that they can shine. In the business world, it seems that sales managers are perhaps the most adept at this. The best of them seem to know how to create a fun, goal-oriented culture that encourages friendly—not cutthroat—competition and inspires every team member to go forth and create a more innovative sales presentation or strengthen the follow-up. It would be great if more Drivers in more departments could take a cue from the sales managers and step up their game.

How are you going to uplift your team today? Would an on-site Zumba class get the blood flowing? Then go out and hire an instructor!

27

Go right to the source
when there is a problem

*Drew's favorite grandmother, Grandma Abigail, used to have a
proverb for every occasion, and her little sayings always seemed
to come back to Drew when he had a difficult situation to
handle. Sometimes, it was like Grandma Abigail was standing
right next to him, giving him advice. Today was one of those
times. He wasn't sure why the bus was dented from end to end
and covered in mud as if it had rolled down a hillside—but
he strongly suspected it had something to do with Rufus's well
documented need for speed. His first inclination was to gather*

the whole team together and demand an explanation from every single one of them. But then he heard Grandma Abigail's sweet voice in his head, repeating one of her favorite sayings: When you don't know what made the carriage tip over, go right to the source and ask the horse. *So Drew took a deep breath. "Rufus, can I have a moment alone with you?"*

If you have a problem with someone on your team, go directly to that person and ask to speak with him. Start out by explaining how something has made you feel, without accusing him of doing something wrong. I suggest starting the conversation by saying, "I respect you, and I wanted to come to you directly instead of mentioning this to anyone else." It's much more respectful that way. And if you don't have the courage to go directly to the source, then you need to keep that person's name and the situation out of your mouth. If you're not going to handle the situation like a professional, then don't compound the problem by spreading your unhappiness and issues. As we all know, the absolute worst way to handle the situation is to go and tell everyone you're close with on the staff about a problem you've noticed. When I see this, it gets on my nerves to no end, because it spreads negativity and it shifts a weight onto the shoulders of those who are trying to run. When you tell all your colleagues about a sticky issue, you are adding weight to them that they don't need.

I once worked with a teacher who went around to everyone, unburdening herself by describing everything that bothered her. She was always in everyone else's space, and when people would ask me where she was, I used to think to myself, *Anywhere but her office*. I would walk around the school and find her hunched over, sitting closely to a staff member, and it was obvious she was unloading all of her problems on them. Honestly, I had to write her up because her work wasn't getting completed. I could tell she was complaining about the fact that I had written her up, but if she had just stopped using her time to complain, she easily could have gotten her work done. When I met with her, I asked her to stop going to talk to the other staff members about her issues, and she said, "I am just asking them for advice." She didn't get it. She couldn't see that she was placing her burdens on the entire staff and by making everyone feel sorry for her, it put a big downer on the organization. As previously stated, people are more than willing to let you be their sponge.

So, in short, if you have an issue to resolve, don't go to all of your colleagues to ask for help. Go directly to anyone you have an issue with, whether it's the boss or otherwise. Be respectful, get to the point, and squash it. If you hold on to the issue, you can't run because it will be holding you down, and you don't want to walk around your organization putting the burden on others either.

28

Show appreciation

Drew has a special rapport with his team. He isn't big on commercialized events, like Employee Appreciation Day, but he makes sure he says thank you several times a day, to each and every person on the bus. For Drew, showing approval is like money in the bank—he can see the effect it has on everyone, the way it makes their eyes shine and their faces light up. Lately, since his team is working harder than ever and has made so many significant gains, Drew is looking for more and more creative ways to show gratitude, and to personalize his gestures. Homemade macadamia nut snickerdoodle cookies are the perfect way to thank Rufus for a job well done, while Joan absolutely melts when he writes her a

poem to express his appreciation. Everyone is different. Ap-
preciation is important.

My grandmother always said, "He who doesn't thank for a little won't thank for a lot." Her point was that if you don't show appreciation for the little things people do for you, those people are unlikely to make a larger effort on your behalf. Showing appreciation is one of the ways you can uplift your staff, which helps to keep everyone performing at a high level.

At RCA, we will occasionally provide lunch or breakfast for the staff. Sometimes we organize surprises or allow staff to leave early for the day. One day the team showed up for professional development, but when they arrived at the meeting room Kim Bearden (the cofounder of RCA) and I were not there. We had left in our stead a simple red envelope that said Open Me. Inside was a word puzzle the team had to solve. Once they did so, the answer led them somewhere else inside our school where another clue was hidden. This went on and on for about an hour, and by that time the team was working together, cheering each other on, and having a blast solving the clues. The final note listed an address with the words, "Come find us." The address led them to Macy's department store, and Kim and I were out front, ready and waiting. When the team approached us, we gave a speech about how deeply appreciative we were for all their hard work and efforts, and then we announced that each person was receiving a shopping trip to Macy's to buy professional clothing. "LET'S GO SHOPPING!" It was an electric moment, and since we ask our staff to dress in business attire every single day, this was a way to show appreciation through a fun outing, as well as to support their efforts to dress for success.

The entire staff jumped and cried and hugged us. They were so appreciative, and it was beautiful.

He who doesn't thank for a little won't thank for a lot.

But then, a few of the staff made a couple of comments that struck me the wrong way—they seemed appreciative, yet they seemed hard to please. One person asked why we had limited the shopping spree to Macy's. Another was so excited that she had tears in her eyes, but then she asked if it was okay to shop for casual clothing as well. Now, the whole point of the experience was so that everyone could have new, fresh attire to wear at RCA, where we have to be in suit and tie every day. I explained it was only for business clothes, and the team member said she completely understood. But, again, it didn't sit well with me. One staff member said she'd rather come back on another day to shop instead of looking at the same time as everyone else; but the point was for us all to shop together and have an electric shopping spree to bond the team. It turned out to be frustrating. When I was planning our staff appreciation activities for the next year, I scratched through the shopping spree idea. I just didn't want to do it again, because those little moments stuck with me and kept me from wanting to create that particular experience again for anyone else. I think it's essential to keep in mind that when someone does something for you, you should make sure to show appreciation quickly and deeply. If not, not only will you be keeping yourself from receiving that type of treatment again but you could also be denying it for others as well.

When you do show appreciation, however, the rewards can be great. I had a teacher from a school who visited RCA email me to tell me that her principal put donut holes in their boxes as a treat. She said she went up to her principal, looked her in the eyes, and let her know that the little treat meant a lot to her. Then she added, "And the next week, we got muffins!"

Everyone on the team needs to understand that how they respond and show appreciation will dictate whether or not those types of experiences will happen for them again. Some employees will complain and complain about how they don't get raises, bonuses, or other perks, but if they look back to moments in the past, they can often correlate their reactions to the future outcomes.

I'll always remember one of our staff members, Gina Coss, at the shopping spree. She kept coming up to me and saying, "Ron? A thousand dollars? It's too much, it's just too much." She was so grateful. She asked if she could use some of her money to help get clothes for RCA students who were in need. I told her that it was just for her. She asked if she could share some of her money with other staff members, and again, I explained that it was a special treat for her. She was so happy and overwhelmed by the kindness. When an entire staff handles themselves in the professional and humble manner of Gina Coss, the depths to which a leader will try to do more and more and more for them can rarely be reached.

29

Enjoy the ride

It is one of those exceptional days on the bus. The sun is shining, the road is clear, and everyone is in perfect step with everyone else. The team is singing Broadway show tunes, which soon give way to old Beatles tunes, and then Rufus starts belting out "We Are the Champions." Joan follows that up with "Y.M.C.A.," complete with arm movements, so everyone will have a chance to stretch. With every chorus, the arm movements get more elaborate and a little sillier—until everyone is laughing. It makes Drew happy to see his team so engaged and in perfect harmony with one another. It's almost as if the bus has just gotten a fresh coat of paint, *he thinks.*

Close your eyes and visualize a kindergarten classroom. I can easily guess what you're picturing in your mind, because all over the world kindergartens are bright, colorful, joyful places designed to spark a child's imagination. But as we go up through the grades, classrooms become progressively more subdued, until by high school we're looking at beige walls and a whiteboard or two. Where did we get this idea that growing up should equate to serious, somber, joyless environments?

At RCA, we've worked very hard to make our school a vibrant, playful, and magical place—not only for our students, but for our staff and visitors as well. Way back in the planning stages, I was determined to create a space that was completely different from any other school on the planet. We have a giant blue slide that connects the second floor to the first-floor lobby, and all our visiting educators are urged to become "slide certified" before they leave. To enter my classroom, you have to activate a sliding bookcase that reveals a secret passage—just like in the cartoon *Scooby-Doo*. I've given my staff wide latitude and a generous budget for decorating their own classrooms as well, in ways that reflect their personalities and style. We have a classroom with a glamorous Hollywood theme. A classroom that's a Moroccan village. A classroom with a Superman phone booth. The entire school reflects the creativity and forward thinking that we apply to everything we do.

If you want your staff to put in extra hours, to show up early and stay late, then you have to allow them to create an environment that makes them feel inspired and productive. Let them paint their walls; paint is cheap, but the impact is priceless. If they don't have walls, then let them paint or draw on their upholstered cubicle dividers. Encourage them to decorate the inside of the bus in a way that lifts them up and helps them to meet their mission. People need to be surrounded by art and toys and objects they love. The tech companies in Silicon Valley and elsewhere seem to have embraced this notion of making the workplace more fun. Pixar even keeps a fleet of scooters at its headquarters and the staff can zoom down the hallways to a meeting.

Other companies are less willing to think outside the box or color outside the lines at all. A friend of mine who worked for a Fortune 500 company wasn't allowed to change out her desk chair for a more ergonomic style. It was actually a company policy that every worker at the same level had to have the same chair. So the organization wanted her to work hard and stay into the evening but didn't want her to be comfortable there or to have lumbar support. It's a mixed message, and it can feel demoralizing to employees.

In one of my favorite movies, *9 to 5*, characters played by Dolly Parton, Lily Tomlin, and Jane Fonda go to extreme lengths to make their workplace a more comfortable and inviting place: they kidnap the boss and hold him prisoner while they redecorate the office and add any number of personal touches. It was hilarious on the big screen, but trust me, you don't want your employees to reach a similar level of desperation!

So you can improve the ride by improving the physical environment. But there's also a mind-set at RCA that we're going to laugh and have fun at work. We have encouraged our staff to joke and laugh often with one another and in front of the students. We want the kids to see that they are in a joyful place with adults who appreciate and like each other. I was giving a speech in front of the entire school and two hundred visiting educators. I bent over during one of my stories, and my pants ripped straight down the back, and it was an audible rip too. No one said a word, but by the looks on everyone's faces it was obvious the entire room knew what happened. Then, in the midst of the awkward silence, one of my staff members said, "Big booty Judy," and the entire room burst into laughter. That, quite obviously, was the best way to handle the situation—through laughter. But in a culture where fun and laughter are not embraced, a staff member would never have been so bold as to say that to a supervisor in that situation.

At the end of eighth grade, we always ask our students to list their top five favorite moments at RCA. Inevitably, the list is always riddled with times where we were simply enjoying the company of one another. The students at RCA travel all over the world, but they will list trips in the school vans as their favorite moment, because it is in those moments we laugh, sing, and bond. Last year's class listed one moment consistently. It was a time I was teaching a lesson using yardsticks, and Kim Bearden was observing. I made a joke about Kim's age, and she grabbed one of the yardsticks and chased me around the room. The kids went wild with laughter, and that moment, that simple moment, was listed as one of the top ones—above four years of global travel. Those moments can be magical, and they can happen in your organization too.

But why are those moments so essential? It's because laughter boosts productivity. It makes a task more manageable. It releases endorphins, forges emotional connections, and can encourage more honest communication. When your staff has fun at work, they work together more collaboratively. Every single day at work becomes a team-building activity.

30

Conclusion:
Where do we go from here?

The parable of the bus has shaped my leadership style. It took a while for it all to come together in my mind, but once I saw that there are clear categories of people—Runners, Joggers, Walkers, Riders, and Drivers—who all approach their jobs in different ways, I could apply those insights to my team at RCA. I could empower people to accomplish seemingly impossible goals. I could even bring about wide-scale change on a level that affects not only my teachers and students, but our nation's entire education system—by showing other school administrators how to build their own dream teams and change the culture at their own schools.

Everyone who reads this book will take away something a little bit different and will find different ways to apply the parable to their own goals. Whether you're currently running or walking, it's important to realize that every single person within an organization has a contribution to make. It doesn't matter what job you were hired to do—your contribution matters. You can always find a way to contribute at a higher level and do a better job, even if you were hired to clean the windshield or put air in the tires of the bus. You can fine-tune some of the small details of your job. You can support the Runners, by volunteering to take over some of their basic tasks. You can look for ways to uplift the people around you—your colleagues, customers, clients, business partners, everyone you come into contact with during your workday. At the very least, you can find a way to complain less in order to change the conversation and contribute to a more positive environment.

And if you don't know where to start, please don't underestimate the value of asking someone what you might do differently. You can go to your supervisor and say, "I want to improve. I want to be a better contributor to this organization; could you please give me tips on how I could do things differently?" And if you've made a mistake, remember that you can humble yourself sometimes and say, "I'm sorry. I did not know how to handle it better. If you could help me, next time I'll make sure I get it right." That is a powerful thing, and it will earn you respect within an organization.

If you're the Driver, please don't fall into the trap of doing something the same way forever because that's the way it's always been done. You can always find ways to be a better leader, while using strategies that will further the goals of your organization. Above all else, you can look for ways to better leverage the Runners and not ask them to hide their achievements. Let them run, give them the tools they need to fly.

If you want to inspire everyone on your team, stand up in front of them and tell them this story about the bus. Explain what you want. Describe the type of environment you hope to create. Paint a detailed picture, with specific goals and expectations. And don't forget to equip your staff to meet those expectations. The bottom line is that people can improve and change. They can find their passion and learn better, more effective ways to do things. Businesses can become better places to work when leaders lay out clear expectations. We just need to have the right tools, and that's what this book is trying to do.

When you are with a team of Runners and you are all supporting each other and doing amazing things, it's the best feeling in the world. It's exactly like the "runner's high" that top athletes experience, that biochemical reaction that makes the run feel easier, more exhilarating, maybe even euphoric.

Epilogue

With all the talk of making the bus run, I felt the need to mention that sometimes it's necessary to stop the bus completely, for the right reason.

While visiting South Africa with our eighth graders, thanks to the generosity of Delta Air Lines, we were delivering supplies to schools when we met a young boy named Sisipho. The name means *gift* in Xhosa, and he would prove to be just that. He quickly bonded with one of our most special and brilliant students at RCA, Ryan Marshall. Wherever we went around Soweto, Sisipho found out and met us there. Eventually, we just started picking him up each day, and eventually he started staying the night with our group. Ryan and Sisipho formed a bond and a friendship like I have never seen before, and those two souls from opposite sides of the world became brothers instantly.

When it was time for us to leave Soweto and head to the airport, we were all crying as we waved good-bye to Sisipho. The young boy stood on the side of the road, waving at us with wild abandon as tears streamed down his face. As the bus reached the highway, Ryan exclaimed, "Stop the bus!" I didn't know what was going on, but the driver slammed on the brakes, and Ryan ran out the door and all the way back to Sisipho. He then took off his necklace and placed it around Sisipho's neck, saying, "Keep this for me. I promise to get it from you again someday."

Months later, at Ryan's eighth grade graduation from RCA I told that story. At the end, I pulled Ryan up onstage and promised him that at some point in Sisipho's life I would make sure he made a trip to America in order to reconnect with Ryan. The entire audience got to their feet to applaud the gesture, and Ryan bowed his head in thanks. I then announced, "Ryan, sometimes promises come true sooner than you think! Come on out, Sisipho!"

The young boy ran out from behind the curtains and he and Ryan grabbed each other as the audience gasped and tears flowed. It was a beautiful and powerful moment, and it wouldn't have happened if Ryan hadn't had the courage to know when it was necessary to bring the bus to a complete stop and create a moment. And it's always important in life, whether it is your personal bus or your business bus, to be aware when those types of moments present themselves and to have the bravery to grasp the magical moment and to live it to the fullest.

Sisipho and Ryan had a bond, but we all grew to love Sisipho as our brother. Having him head back to Soweto after the visit was heartbreaking, and the next year when we made our class trip to South Africa, reconnecting with him was one of the most joyous moments of my life. Leaving him again, after ten days, was just too much for all of us to bear. As the bus pulled off that year, we all cried, but when I looked at Kim Bearden, her eyes were dry. I asked, through tears, "Why aren't you crying," and she replied, "I'm adopting him." I said, "*Huh,*" and she responded, "Yup. I am going to go home and tell my husband we are adopting that child."

And she did.

Sisipho now attends RCA, and he is thriving.

Unfortunately, an unspeakable tragedy occurred. During a robbery at Ryan's home, he was shot while trying to shield his mother from the bullet of the robbers. He died in his mother's arms, a hero. An angel.

The world lost someone who was not only kind, generous, and talented, but the world lost someone who was willing to step up, to speak out, and to make major moments happen. He was willing to stop the bus in order to do what was right. His instincts were spot-on. He somehow knew exactly what needed to happen.

Ryan is no longer with us, but what helps me to deal with the loss is that I know I will be running for him. I will be working to make a difference in the lives of others, for him. I will know when to the stop the bus, for him.

My greatest fear is that those of you who are reading this are going to become old and have regrets. You are going to wish you could go back and do things over. I feel that, as long as we live like Ryan and realize the importance of making moments for others, we will be content with the lives we have lived. Ryan's life was cut short at fifteen, but his legacy is changing the life of Sisipho forever. Ryan touched us all in ways that uplifted us, that encouraged us, and that made us want to be better. We all have the power to do that, and when we step up to be that type of person, then we are truly running.

And it is my greatest wish that in his honor, you will all look to make moments for others like Ryan made for Sisipho. Moments where you too can create magic. Moments where you profoundly affect the lives of others. Moments when you are truly running. Moments when you are truly and inexplicably alive. I wish you luck, my friends. Let's change the world.